Tom Nuelson

# Two Presidents

## Abraham Lincoln
## Jefferson Davis

Also by Tom Hudson:

*The West Is My Home*
*Three Paths Along a River*
    plus numerous soft-cover
    books and magazine articles

# Two Presidents

## Abraham Lincoln
## Jefferson Davis

### by C. E. Gilbert

### Introductions, Highlights and Explanations

### by Tom Hudson
#### Editor

**The Naylor Company**
*Book Publishers of the Southwest*
San Antonio, Texas

Library of Congress Cataloging in Publication Data

Gilbert, C          E
    Two presidents: Abraham Lincoln and Jefferson Davis.

    Reprint of the 1927 ed.
    1.  United  States — History — Civil  War — Causes.
2.  Lincoln, Abraham, Pres. U. S., 1809-1865.
3.  Davis, Jefferson, 1808-1889.  I.  Title.
E459.G53   1973                    973.7'092'2    [B]                    73-6581
ISBN  0-8111-0484-2

This edition is dedicated to the
author of the original book.

Charles Edwin Gilbert

# About This Book
# and Its Author

Admittedly, what Charles Edwin Gilbert has to say in this book is biased. By many it will be considered a vicious attack on an honored man. But what you will read is no more biased than are hundreds of other books dealing with that man; the principal difference being that the vast majority of those other books are biased antithetically.

Broken down into the book's components, these points stand out:

The author has placed the blame for the War Between the States on Abraham Lincoln and a few of his advisors, and the cause as violation of States' Rights and armed invasion — not slavery.

The author resents the popular name of the war, Civil War, as being a misnomer because it was fought, not within one country, but between two republics. He also resents the name War of the Rebellion because, once the Southern States had seceded and formed the Confederate States of America, a rebellion against the United States of America was impossible. For the same reason he resents the term *rebel*.

The author points to sentiment among many leaders of the South as favoring freeing of the slaves before the war began, and credits the South with a prominent role in halting the slave traffic.

The author blames Lincoln and his administration with flagrant violation of the Constitution of the United States.

The author points out that Lincoln's proclamation "freeing the slaves" actually did not free a single slave — at least not until the war's end — as the proclamation applied only to the Southern States where Lincoln at that time had no jurisdiction. The author also cites the fact that those border states exempted in the proclamation, and which still condoned slavery, retained their slaves until they were freed by passage of the Thirteenth Amendment seven months after Lee had surrendered at Appomattox Courthouse.

The author stresses the rights of states to secede, and the general acceptance of this right at the time of the War Between the States.

The author has credited Jefferson Davis, President of the Confederacy, with being a patriot, both to the Union and to the Confederacy in turn, of the highest integrity.

And finally, the author asserts that his disclosure of many historical facts contained herein is not done to reopen old wounds, but for the sake of preserving an honest account of history. To put it in his own words on the cover of his original book: "The truth of history belongs to posterity."

In order to fully understand his many references to the Republican and Democratic parties, it should be remembered that in their concepts, these two parties have seemingly reversed themselves since the years of strife of which Gilbert writes.

In this new printing, references usually found at the bottom of the pages have been bracketed and inserted in the text. They contain brief information as to sources with which the reader might not otherwise be familiar. To make this edition more valuable to students of history, an index has been included at the back of the book.

The three short "Highlight" chapters herein are included for convenience in refreshing the reader's memory on the war and upon the two principals who, as commanders in

viii

chief, dictated the war's policy — from the North and from the South.

If you are an average American you will doubtless be shocked many times as you delve into Gilbert's pages, but, if you are earnestly seeking the truth, you will value what he has to say. The sources from which he has drawn speak for themselves.

Now to get acquainted with the author and learn something of his background:

It would be difficult to attempt an introduction of Charles Edwin Gilbert, the man whose comprehensive studies are reflected in the fascinating pages to follow, without at least briefly introducing his father, Capt. Love Gilbert, and his son, Charles E. Gilbert, Jr. All three men have dealt with history — either in the making or in the telling, and in most cases both. It was his father who started Charles Edwin Gilbert on the road he followed, and it is his son who has carried on in his stead.

Capt. Love Gilbert, the author's father, as a weekly newspaper publisher in Alabama recorded history as it happened, and as he saw it in the making. But Love Gilbert was also a *maker* of history. As publisher of the *Jasper Advertiser* in 1861-62 he strongly urged secession of his state from the Union. In the spring of 1862, true to his convictions, he enlisted in the Confederate Army and was elected first lieutenant of a company assigned to the Twenty-eighth Alabama Regiment. Like a vast majority of the men with whom he served, he owned no slaves.

After the Battle of Iuka in Mississippi, in which he participated, he was commissioned as a captain and led his company through the battles of Corinth and Shiloh. He was a part of Gen. Braxton Bragg's army in the campaign through Kentucky and Tennessee and down to Chattanooga. He was in all the hard fighting around Chattanooga — the Battle Above the Clouds, Chickamauga, and Mission Ridge.

At Mission Ridge he was wounded and later in the same day, when ammunition was exhausted, he and his entire company were captured. After a short imprisonment in the Maxwell Hotel in Nashville he was sent to Johnson's Island in Lake Erie where he spent the remainder of the war.

Upon his release from prison in June of 1865, at the age of thirty-four, Capt. Love Gilbert returned to Alabama only to find that his newspaper plant in Jasper had been destroyed by fire on March 27 of that year in what is popularly known as Wilson's Raid, conducted by Gen. James H. Wilson of the Union Army. In the little town of Carrollton in western Alabama, where he had been married, Love Gilbert became publisher of another weekly newspaper, the *West Alabamian*.

It was here that his son, Charles Edwin Gilbert, then ten years of age, started his career in newspaper work; first as "devil," then gradually assuming his role as writer and publisher. Fresh in his mind at that time were the events of the war that had taken his father from him for four years and had cost the life of his mother in the early days of the war. "My mother must have died from starvation and neglect," he later said, "for what I remember most was how hungry I was when Grandma came, and how good the hard biscuit, which she brought with her, tasted."

Always observant, Charles Edwin Gilbert had absorbed many of the sordid details of the war that had pitted North against South and brother against brother. His training in newspaper work sharpened his memory of details; and that same training, later in life, gave him the ability to do extensive research of the events that led to, promoted and carried the war through four of America's most perilous years.

Twelve years after his father had become publisher of the *West Alabamian*, Charles Edwin Gilbert migrated to Texas where, in 1877, he established the weekly *Navasota Tablet* in South Texas. In 1881 he moved to the frontier town of Abilene — composed mostly of tents — and established the *Abilene Reporter,* the first of his newspapers to find permanency.

While Abilene and the *Reporter* grew and prospered, Charles Edwin Gilbert, his father's pioneering blood thick in his veins, looked about him and decided that the burgeoning town of Dallas, to the east, was destined to be a great city. So, in 1889 he went to Dallas and soon acquired both the *Dallas Evening Times* and the *Dallas Herald.* He consolidated the two papers, thus founding the *Dallas Times-Herald,* today one of the South's great newspapers.

His later years were spent in Houston, with occasional trips to Washington and through the South. It was on these trips, and in Houston, that he assembled much of the material for this book.

In appearance and in demeanor Charles Edwin Gilbert was a true Southern gentleman. If he were living today he would be hailed as a "Kentucky Colonel" of the highest rank. I best remember him when, as a boy, I sat across my mother's table from him and listened in wide-eyed wonder to his rapid and learned conversation — all the while his white beard bobbing up and down as he consumed quantities of small crusty buttermilk biscuits hot out of the wood-stove oven and beautifully browned fried chicken brought in heaps from an iron skillet on the same kitchen stove.

As his beard grew longer and whiter — but never less well groomed — Charles Edwin Gilbert's interests reverted to the great events that had so affected his youth. Deeper and deeper he delved into the true history of the War Between the States and the two men who had headed the two rival republics engaged in that war. At last, in 1927, he was ready to let the world know the results of his studies. Unfortunately, the book he printed under the title *Two Presidents: Abraham Lincoln, Jefferson Davis; Origin, Cause and Conduct of the War Between the States,* was a limited paperback edition and its readers were far too few.

In this new edition, published forty-five years later, the author's original words are retained, but the format has been modernized. Appropriate pictures have been used to lend interest and reality.

Charles Edwin Gilbert's son, Charles E. Gilbert, Jr., has followed in the footsteps of his grandfather and father. It is to him that we are grateful for permission to republish his father's book. For many years he was editor of *Houston*, the official publication of the Houston Chamber of Commerce and the largest such publication in the nation. Retiring from that arduous task, he, also, turned to history and is author of several books dealing with Texas history. Four years ago, then at the age of eighty-one, he wrote to me that he was completing and getting ready for publication a history of the city of Houston.

It is with pride that I introduce these three historians as: Capt. Love Gilbert, *Grandpa Gilbert*; Charles Edwin Gilbert, author of the book, *Uncle Charley*; and Charles E. Gilbert, Jr., *Cousin Charles*.

Tom Hudson

# Some Highlights of the War Between the States (The Civil War)

The cause of the War Between the States had its origin in Colonial days, before the War of Independence. The economy of the South was built on agriculture with its resultant widespread use of slaves, while that of the North was built more on industry and shipping, including the importation of slaves until the slave traffic was outlawed in 1820.

This difference in the economic backgrounds of the two sections of the country gradually increased during the years and reached its climax when South Carolina seceded from the Union on December 20, 1860, soon to be followed by ten other states. The Confederate States of America was organized at Montgomery, Alabama, its capital established at Richmond, Virginia, and attempts made to settle differences with the Union were to no avail.

On April 11, 1861, Union Naval forces occupied Fort Pickens at Pensacola, Florida, and two days later attempted to land supplies and reinforcements for Fort Sumter at Charleston, South Carolina. Southern troops fired on the fort and the verbal war had become a shooting war — a war that was to cost the lives of 529,492 men, only 3,297 less than were lost in all American wars from the American

Revolution up to and including World War II. And this figure does not include the uncounted thousands of helpless men, women and children who died of malnutrition, broken homes and broken hearts. The first blood was shed at Baltimore on April 19 when Union forces were attacked by a mob.

The South had its first great victory on July 21 of that year at the First Battle of Bull Run (also known as Manassas) in Virginia. For almost two years following this Southern victory the South, even though far outnumbered, continued to win more battles than it lost. With its enormous output of cotton, upon which England depended to keep its mills running, the South, in spite of a Northern blockade, managed to carry on its commerce with European countries and thereby obtain the necessities of war. In fact, the South nurtured a hope that England would come to her aid militarily.

Until this time the question of slavery had never been proclaimed as a cause of the war. Then, on January 1, 1863, Lincoln issued his Proclamation of Emancipation (of Southern slaves only) and all hopes of the South for active help from England came to an end. The European nations simply refused to take any part in a war which, through Lincoln's proclamation, had overnight ostensibly become a war over slavery.

The turning point in the war came forcefully a few months later when Union forces were victorious in the Battle of Gettysburg in Pennsylvania and at Vicksburg in Mississippi. The Union victory at Vicksburg cut the Mississippi River in two and in effect won much of the Southern territory for the North.

Outnumbered on all sides, Gen. Robert E. Lee surrendered to Gen. U. S. Grant at Appomattox Courthouse on April 9, 1865. Other Southern forces quickly followed suit.

# Contents

Jefferson Davis

# Some Highlights in the Life of Jefferson Davis

The future President of the Confederate States of America and one of the most controversial men in American history, Jefferson Davis, was born in Kentucky on June 3, 1808. In 1828, at the age of twenty, he graduated from West Point and subsequently served seven years in the United States Army. Failing to find the stimulation he needed, he resigned his commission as lieutenant in 1835 and married Sarah Knox Taylor, daughter of Col. (later President) Zachary Taylor. She died three months later and for the next ten years Davis was a planter in Mississippi. As a plantation owner he gave to his slaves a measure of self-government wherein they had their own jury system.

In 1844 Davis served as a Democratic presidential elector, and one year later was elected to the United States House of Representatives. In that same year, 1845, he again married, this time to Varina Howard, granddaughter of Gov. Richard Howell of New Jersey.

His duties as a Congressman were soon interrupted when the Mexican War started in 1846 and Davis resigned his Congressional seat to become colonel of the First Mississippi Infantry. He served with such brilliance in and around Monterrey — where his maneuvering saved the day for his former father-in-law, Zachary Taylor — that President Polk offered him a commission as a brigadier general. This he refused because, he said, the President did not have the Constitutional right to make the appointment.

Having been wounded at Buena Vista, he returned to his Mississippi home, but the following year was appointed to the United States Senate. In that position he soon became chairman of the committee on military affairs.

In 1851 he made a try for the governorship of Mississippi, but was defeated.

Two years later, in 1853, he became Secretary of War under Pres. Franklin Pierce, a position he held for four years. Among his accomplishments were enlargement of the army, direction of surveys for a railroad to the Pacific, betterment of conditions at West Point, and inauguration of a military camel service across the arid Southwestern United States, a move that he hoped would fill in the gap that was to precede the building of a railroad.

In 1857 Davis reentered the United States Senate where he worked diligently for States' Rights. He had always been a staunch believer in the rights of states to secede, and when his own state seceded in 1861 following the election of Abraham Lincoln as President, Davis made his farewell speech to the Senate and returned to the South. He was immediately chosen as Provisional President of the Confederacy and was inaugurated at Montgomery, Alabama, and, later that year, at Richmond, Virginia.

He attempted to negotiate withdrawal of Union forces in Southern forts, but failed. Failure of this effort soon resulted in the firing at Fort Sumter and the war was on. Its conduct in the interest of the South was to be his responsibility for the next four years.

With the evacuation of Richmond in 1865, and collapse of Southern resistance, he moved the Confederate executive offices to Danville, Virginia, then to Greensboro, North Carolina. In an attempt to join forces with trans-Mississippi holdouts, he was captured near Irwinville, Georgia, on May 10, 1865, and confined in manacles at Fortress Monroe,

Virginia. For two years before being released, he was held under threat of trial for treason.

He retired to Belvoir, Mississippi, and died in New Orleans on December 6, 1889. He is buried at Richmond, Virginia.

Abraham Lincoln

# Some Highlights in the Life of Abraham Lincoln

Like Jefferson Davis, Abraham Lincoln was born in Kentucky, and less than a year separated the two men's births. Both grew physically to well beyond a slender height of six feet. Both men served in the Black Hawk War and both later served as Presidents of their respective republics during the same four years. Both carried on their backs the burden of a war that affected the lives of the same millions of people.

It would seem that, with these similarities, Lincoln and Davis might have been cast in the same mold. But, on the contrary, there the similarity ended.

Lincoln was reared in poverty. At an early age his family moved to Indiana and then to Illinois. While Davis was graduating from West Point, Lincoln had managed only about one year of formal education.

In his early years Lincoln worked as a laborer, as a clerk in a store, and as a surveyor. However, he bettered his education through determined self-teaching and, in 1832, made an unsuccessful attempt at the Illinois State Legislature, at the same time serving as elected captain of a company of volunteers in the Black Hawk War — a war in which his company was never engaged in conflict.

Two years later he was elected to the State Legislature

and in 1842 was married to Mary Todd. During these years he practiced law and served as a local leader in the Whig party, again meeting defeat when he ran for Congress in 1843.

His ambition to serve in Washington was finally realized in 1847 when he was elected to Congress. His two-year term — he was defeated for reelection — was marked principally by a bill he introduced providing for emancipation of slaves in the District of Columbia with consent of the voters and with compensation to slave owners. The bill was never considered in Congress.

Returning to Illinois he was offered the governorship of the new Territory of Oregon. At the insistence of his wife he refused the offer. From 1849 to 1854 he practiced law in Illinois and for the first time in his life knew a degree of prosperity.

A turning point in his life seems to have come when he was invited to reply to a speech made by Stephen A. Douglas. The Kansas-Nebraska Act had opened the Northwest Territory to slavery and Douglas had supported the act. Lincoln's reply to Douglas, on October 16, 1854, had such wide acclaim that, overnight, Lincoln became a national figure. As a result of this popularity he ran as a Whig candidate for a seat in the Senate. Again he was defeated.

Lincoln joined the new Republican party and, in 1858, as a candidate for Senate on the Republican ticket, took part in the famous series of debates with Douglas who was seeking the Senatorial seat on the Democratic ticket. Once more — and for the last time — Lincoln was defeated.

The search by Republicans for a candidate who could carry Western, as well as Eastern, votes for President, resulted in Lincoln's nomination and, although he received a minority popular vote, in 1860 he became the sixteenth President of the United States.

His refusal to withdraw Union forces from Southern forts, but instead to reinforce the forts, precipitated the war.

One of the most noteworthy of his political actions in

office was the Proclamation of Emancipation, officially issued on January 1, 1863, wherein all slaves in Southern States were theoretically freed.

He was reelected in 1864 and on April 14, 1865, was assassinated by John Wilkes Booth in Ford's Theatre in Washington. He is buried at Springfield, Illinois.

# Two Presidents

## Abraham Lincoln
## Jefferson Davis

## Origin, Cause and Conduct
## of the War Between the States

## by
## C. E. Gilbert

All notes enclosed in brackets are the editor's

# Introduction

In my work for several years through the South I have had occasion to observe and lament the lack of historical information among young people of the present generation, even among grown-ups, and the extent of alleged history which, through misrepresentation, serves to discredit our fathers and deprive them of the honors justly due them. There is some reason for this condition:

The cause which impoverished the South in the 1860s enriched the North; and while the men of the South must return home in the spring of '65 and devote years of hard work to rehabilitating the Southland, men of the North had money and leisure to write, print and misrepresent the cause and conduct of that terrible conflict.

There is reason in everything which has any basis at all. There is a reason why it is just to assert that Pres. Abraham Lincoln's fame is far beyond the man's deserts; his abilities exaggerated; his virtues magnified; his statesmanship overestimated; his one achievement misrepresented and misunderstood, conflictive in declaration, purpose and effect.

All this would be immaterial but for the propaganda of misrepresentation of issues and policies, having tendency and purpose to deceive those who thoughtlessly accept

1

them. If those policies and actions which forced that war upon the South were false and wrong, then, certainly, Southern people insult the memory of their fathers in permitting the circulation in their homes and schools of such literature.

Southern people are not concerned about the exaggerated adulation of Lincoln in the North, or the hero-worship by the negroes of the South as long as they wish to be deluded; but it is the wrongful use of their publishing advantage — the circulation of misrepresentations and calumnies at our own doors — that merits our indignant protest. What would be the reception accorded a proposal to name a Southern female college for Harriet Beecher Stowe after her gross misrepresentation of Southern life? Or if it were proposed to name a high school for John Brown or Wendell Phillips, both of whom were early proponents to destroy the Federal Constitution in order to create negro insurrection and bring about negro equality — only in the South?

[Harriet Beecher Stowe, author of *Uncle Tom's Cabin*, published in 1852 and credited with being a factor in events leading to the war. . . . John Brown, American abolitionist and leader of the attack on Harpers Ferry, Virginia, in 1859. Convicted of treason and murder and hanged. . . . Wendell Phillips, lawyer, author and abolitionist.]

Well, Lincoln claimed the power, and did what these fanatics had suggested. Is there a school in Massachusetts or Ohio named in honor of Jefferson Davis or Robert E. Lee? Has not Northern sentiment kept out of the Hall of Fame the statue of Jefferson Davis — out of the niche set apart for Mississippi?

While the men of the South displayed their characteristic courage and fortitude, in the one field as in the other,

2

and were remarkably successful in restoring their homes and industries to their former glory and productiveness — it required many years, and there was little time for literature — the conquerors went marching on writing and printing versions of events which should have been recorded with something of the impartiality of a magnanimous victor, but instead were prejudiced, unjust and untrue. The saddest phase of this period, so akin to the destructive political "reconstruction," is that during these crippled years of the South such books in innumerable numbers found their way almost alone into the homes and schools of the South with their venomous influences.

It may be our fault — certainly our misfortune — that so many of our young are unfamiliar with the official record of either of the war Presidents, or the heroic parts their ancestors played in that eventful period of our country's history; and consequently are unable to form correct judgment. But they are entitled to know the truth, and we owe it to our fathers that their descendants shall know the truth — all the truth.

There is ample and valid reason for disbelieving and in repudiating hundreds of the books written (for gain and hate) in the years following President Lincoln's tragic and lamentable assassination. Lincoln was the new Republican party's first President. Lincoln, dead and discredited (as he had been for a year), would mean the death of the new Republican party; but Lincoln, famous and reputed great in achievement, would mean extended life to the party.

So, the President's administration must be extolled, his every act exalted, his personality magnified to the greatest extent; the South must be charged with Lincoln's death; the Southern States must be ground down and "reconstructed"; Jefferson Davis must be charged with complicity in Lincoln's death, and with responsibility for the death rate at Andersonville. There must be victims; Mrs. Surratt dragged from her home and hanged with men charged

3

with Lincoln's death, and Superintendent [Henry] Wirz of Andersonville hanged [on November 10, 1865] by military court; Jefferson Davis placed in a cell and in irons — thus carrying out the plan of Wendell Phillips' Republican party: "organization against the South" to "trample the Constitution under foot."

[Andersonville Prison was a Confederate prisoner-of-war camp at the village of Andersonville, Georgia, used from February, 1864 to April, 1865. . . . Mrs. Mary E. Surratt was convicted as one of the conspirators in the assassination of Abraham Lincoln and hanged on July 7, 1865.]

Hundreds of books were written voicing the most extravagant adulation of the dead President, and those which dared tell some of the truth were bought up and suppressed; particularly those of W. H. Herndon and Ward Lamon [U.S. Marshal for the District of Columbia], who, though Republicans and former law partners and intimate friends of Lincoln, "could not tell the truth," because they did not participate in the apotheosis of a man dead who had been so recently denounced by his associates while living. Even Mr. [Salmon Portland] Chase, Lincoln's appointee from the Cabinet to Chief Justice of the Supreme Court, who admitted his Republican party devotion was not for love of the negro so much as hate for his master, said he "could never see any greatness in Lincoln."

These are the reasons for the presentation of this volume, that it may be an humble but helpful means of disseminating some of the much hidden truths. In offering it, I beg to call attention to one feature of it: Ninety percent of the authorities quoted to show the gross inaccuracy and injustice of the mass of so-called history in circulation are from Northern historians, newspapers and public men in the Northern States before, during and since the war, and also from that other invaluable collection of war

4

records authorized by act of Congress in the name of *Records of the War of the "Rebellion."* We can pardon the name for the truth it tells.

C. E. Gilbert

# I

# Two Presidents

It was Macaully who said "A people who are not proud of the deeds of a noble ancestry will never do anything worthy to be remembered by posterity."

It is the sacred duty of Southerners, and should be their blessed privilege to contribute whatever is within their means or power for the preservation of the truth of history to the honor and memory of the Confederate soldiers and statesmen. Our fathers of '61 fought valiantly to preserve and perpetuate the principles won by our heroic ancestors of '76 and true Americans should delight to honor the one no less than the other. The truth of history, of the striking events of that period — the simple truth — is all the sons and daughters of the Confederacy desire, and *that* we should insist be taught in our schools and in the homes throughout the Southland. Failure to do so, neglect to do our full part, would be a shame which should lose us the respect even of descendants of the men who wore the blue.

Even fair-minded men of the Northern States would no doubt gladly welcome suggestions which would lead to the full truth on that important epoch in the history of our country — not for any material advantage, or fear of any false sentiment, but for the sake of Truth itself.

In this presentation of the record of the two central figures in the War Between the States, I make no pretense at either "literature" or eloquence, but endeavor to present truths of history in an effort to show fairly and truly the efforts and influence of the one to preserve the Union and avoid war by a strict adherence to the Constitution, and statutes, and to adjust existing and perplexing problems by peaceful means; and of the other to override law and Constitution to bring on war, for what Seward termed "the higher law," which was revolution reversed, official rebellion against the people.

[William H. Seward served as Governor of New York, in the United States Senate, and as Secretary of State under Lincoln.]

Jefferson Davis was a man of ability, stability of character and of the strictest integrity — a man who studied public questions, could quickly analyze perplexing problems, and whose conclusions were wise and unchanging. He was not a man of vacillating mind, favoring a measure today and condemning it tomorrow, nor the kind of politician who changes his position with every shifting wind. Because of his ability and wisdom and the purity of his character, he had the confidence of the South and was a trusted leader. His entire public career showed an ambition for service, unswerving devotion to democratic principles — a desire to be useful to his country and helpful to fellowmen; and in that, his life was a marked success.

What was the cause of the War Between the States? The Northern writers generally say slavery. But the origin and the cause date back to a period when slavery was in existence North and South.

7

There was rivalry and jealousy and growing enmity between the Puritan and the Cavalier, starting probably when New England failed in reciprocation to come to the aid of Virginia in her Indian wars, or perhaps to the inherent and inharmonious characteristics of Puritan and Cavalier.

In 1775, this feeling between the two sections was recognized by Gen. George Washington, when, at Boston, he issued a stern order for the summary punishment of any man guilty of arousing that sectional animosity.

In 1776, John Jay, as Secretary of Foreign Affairs, recommended to Congress in the treaty with Spain there should be no American shipping on the Mississippi River below the mouth of the Yazoo, which brought forth strong protests from Virginia and other Southern States.

In 1803, the North protested against Pres. Thomas Jefferson's purchase of Louisiana, and yet strongly contended for control of the Northwest Territory thereby admitted to the Union.

In 1812, the Northern section protested and criticized the Southern States for the war with England which, by the way, was won almost altogether by Southern men.

In 1814, New England representatives in the Hartford [Connecticut] Convention threatened secession because of the war with England.

In 1820, Congress, on motion of Thomas Jefferson, and by the vote of Southern members, passed an act prohibiting the slave traffic, which stopped a very profitable trade in New England shipbuilding and kidnapping of Africans. It was then the Abolition sentiment received its first impetus.

In 1828, Congress, the Northern section again in control, raised tariff taxes on imports for the protection of New England mills to an extent which brought forth vigorous protest from the South that Congress had exceeded the powers delegated by the states, which brought forth the Nullification Act of South Carolina in 1832. Though President Jackson threatened, under the leadership of Clay,

Congress modified the tariff, and South Carolina repealed the Nullification Act in 1833.

> [Prior to the war, through a strict interpretation of the U.S. Constitution, any state could nullify a Federal law within its boundaries if the State Legislature considered that the Federal government had, in passing the law, overstepped the authority delegated to it by the States. . . . Henry Clay, American statesman, served in the House of Representatives and Senate, and as Secretary of State under John Quincy Adams.]

In 1846-1847, Massachusetts took the lead in protest against the Mexican War and threatened to withdraw from the Union if Texas was admitted; and sought to control the new territory won by Southern valour while they were protesting.

In 1859, the Northern States annulled extradition laws, and not only refused to surrender fugitive slaves, but Ohio and Iowa openly refused to honor the requisition of the Governor of Virginia for two of John Brown's raiders who were indicted with Brown for murder in Virginia.

In 1860, there came another national victory for the Northern States (on account of three Democratic presidential tickets) in the election of Abraham Lincoln and both Houses of Congress. With Wendell Phillips, one of the founders of the new Republican party, declaring the party was "a sectional party organized against the South" to "trample the Constitution under foot," and S. P. Chase, in Lincoln's cabinet and his spokesman in the Peace Conference, declaring there would be no compromise and that Lincoln's election authorized him to "enforce his theories regardless of Constitution, laws, State Rights or Supreme Court" — we have a culmination of the long-growing enmity for the South, an open hostility menacing the peace of the South.

[Virginia, the last state to secede, before seceding called for a peace conference at Washington. The conference failed to stem the tide toward war.]

What was left for the Southern States, except to do what New England had often threatened to do — withdraw from the Union?

Judge James Taylor Bledsoe in his *Origin of the Late War* said: "The causes of the late war had their roots in the passions of the human heart. Thus the new government worked, not according to physical analogies, but according to the principles of human nature. The weak looked to the Constitution as the great charter of their rights; the powerful looked to their own power. The minority held up the shield of State Rights; the majority laid its hand on the sword of the Union. The only difference is, that in thus passing from the creed (State Rights) and the attitude (threatening secession) of the minority, to those of the majority and back again, according to her change of position and power in the Union, new England has been more bold and unblushing than any other portion of the United States; and at the same time more lofty in her pretensions to a purely disinterested patriotism and loyalty."

After discussing at length the efforts at provision for a balance of power between small and large states by equal representation in one House and proportionate representation in the other, and a balance of power between the two Houses, and the legislative, executive and judicial departments, with the Supreme Court as final arbiter, Judge Bledsoe said: "The failure to adjust or settle on any solid basis the balance of power between the North and South was the great defect of the Constitution of 1787. Hence, if we are not greatly mistaken, the antagonism between the North and South so imperfectly adjusted by the labors of 1787, is the true standpoint from which to contemplate the origin of the late war."

10

Thus, it should be clearly understood that the antagonism was before strife over the tariff, and was growing in intensity before division over slavery. The North could not afford to make the tariff a war issue for that would have incurred the displeasure and opposition of Great Britain; so slavery was made their pretext for war, and even that had to be handled very cautiously, for an open issue would have antagonized the Northwest. Lincoln had failed in such an issue with Stephen A. Douglas [See *Some Highlights in the Life of Abraham Lincoln* on preceding pages] over state sovereignty (indirectly involving slavery), and Gen. Ulysses S. Grant [commander of the Union Army and eighteenth President of the United States] had said even after the war was on, that "If this war is for emancipation I will resign, and go take my sword to the other side." So, the movement for war must be secretly and very diplomatically conducted.

Abraham Lincoln was born in Kentucky in 1809, in humble circumstances, raised amid poverty and unenviable surroundings, and consequently deserves credit for application to study and an ambition which brought him from obscurity to great eminence. His early manhood, however, was spent among an undesirable element, in population and environment, which no doubt left its impress upon his character. His boyhood studiousness was praiseworthy, and the ambition of his early manhood commendable — but arriving at maturity his vacillating course politically would seem to indicate that his ambition for prominence overshadowed and submerged the finer qualities and better impulses of the man.

As a youth, his example promised great worth and usefulness, but as a man he seemed to yield himself to the policy or methods which for the time appeared to offer the best aid to his political advancement. Both Herndon and Lamon, who were in later life law partners, and his biographers, state that he chose for his friends the roughest

11

and most ignorant of his acquaintances; and that upon one occasion in his saloon in Salem, Illinois, when one of his friends was worsted in a fight, Lincoln grabbed a whisky bottle by the neck and jumped into the ring, saying: "I am the big buck of this lick, and if anyone here wants to dispute it let him whet his horns and step into the ring." This is quoted merely to show the environment of his early manhood.

It was soon after this that he served in the Black Hawk War, and was elected to the Legislature where he served two terms, and soon thereafter was elected to a seat in Congress. During his term in Congress, the agitation arose over the admission of Texas into the Union during the war with Mexico. Massachusetts was threatening to secede if Texas was admitted, and Lincoln made a speech favoring the right of a state to secede.

About this time a New York member of the House offered a resolution expressing strong opposition to the war with Mexico, and denouncing it as "unjust and unconstitutional" (almost treasonable), and in supporting the resolution the author made the remarkable declaration that "he hoped the American Army would find a bloody welcome and hospitable graves." Lincoln voted for the resolution, following such a declaration, his most conspicuous act in the House; and yet, fifteen years later, he forced a war more "unjust and unconstitutional" against a section of his own country, without any authority whatever.

There are two great and vital points which cannot be ignored, must be understood — two great principles — underlying the cause of the War Between the States:

1. The right of secession — whatever the cause — though slavery was not, only the excuse.

2. The right of self-defense — the right to repel armed invasion.

The right of secession was reserved by the states in the organization of the Republic, and acknowledged through

12

the North, yea, claimed and threatened by all of the New England States in the Hartford Convention in 1814 and again by Massachusetts in 1846 in her protest against the admission of Texas. It was openly conceded in public print and public speeches through the North as late as 1861, by Lincoln in the House in 1847, even indirectly in the Republican platform of 1860. The right, then, should be conceded now by every fair man.

Then, as to the right of the South to fire on Fort Sumter: After months of delay in the evacuation of the fort by the Federal garrison; Lincoln's instructions to Major [Robert] Anderson to hold the fort, he would send reinforcements; repeated promises of Lincoln and Seward to withdraw the garrison, and their violation of the pledges; their equipment of a relief squadron, and appearance of the reinforcement fleet off Charleston after South Carolina had peacefully and formally seceded and was a state of the duly organized Confederate States — was purely an act of self-defense; as, had Fort Sumter been occupied by Federal reinforcements, the next move would be on Charleston.

Horace Greeley said in 1861: "If the Declaration of Independence justified the three million colonists in 1776, I do not see why the Constitution ratified by the same men should not justify the secession of six million Southerners in 1861."

John Quincy Adams in 1839 made an elaborate argument in favor of the right of secession of the state, while Josiah Quincy made the first claim in Congressional halls to the right of secession in 1811.

Benjamin J. Williams of Massachusetts, in his book *Died for His State,* said of the right of secession reserved by the states, that "Each state has the right to judge for itself if the infraction of the Federal government is sufficient to warrant her withdrawal."

*New York Herald,* November 11, 1860: "The South has the undeniable right to secede from the Union. In the event of secession, the City of New York and New Jersey will go with them."

Benjamin T. Wade, of Ohio: "Who is the arbiter of that right? Why, to yield the right of the state to withdraw" would be to "submit to a miserable despotism."

[Horace Greeley, founder of the *New York Tribune*, member of Congress, author, and anti-slavery leader. . . . Josiah Quincy, statesman, orator, historian. Served as Congressman from Massachusetts. . . . Benjamin T. Wade, U.S. Senator from Ohio 1861-1869. Acting Vice-President under Pres. Andrew Johnson after Lincoln's assassination.]

In 1847 Lincoln believed in the right of secession, and spoke in favor of it, but in 1861 opposed it. At Peoria, Illinois, in 1854 he said, "The slaveholder has a moral and legal right to his slaves." In 1857 he said that the negro was an inferior being and would never be fit for citizenship. At Chicago and Springfield, Illinois, in 1858, he took the position in debate with Douglas that the negro was equal to the white man and, as he claimed, "entitled to equal rights as declared by the Declaration of Independence"; but in his response to Judge Douglas in South Illinois (settled by people from the South) he strenuously endeavored to deny this and explained or modified his criticism of a Supreme Court decision that "the negro could never be a citizen." Yet, Lincoln's proclamation in 1863 was designed to start the negro on to citizenship, 100,000 of them being enlisted in the Federal Army at his instance.

In that memorable debate Douglas often tried to get Lincoln to repeat in South Illinois utterances of his in Northern Illinois, and vice versa — so contradictory were his speeches in the two sections. While Illinois was Anti-State-Sovereignty and Lincoln made his campaign for Senator on that issue (though dodging it in South Illinois) he was defeated by Douglas, largely because of his varying and conflicting utterances.

14

When the leaders of the new Republican party came to look for a candidate for President, they concluded that William H. Seward of New York, and others, were so partisan neither could carry the West. "Any nominee could carry Pennsylvania, New York and New England," they urged, "but a western man is necessary to carry the states west of Ohio." So Lincoln as a man who would appeal to the West and the labor (Democratic) vote of the cities was agreed on and nominated at Chicago.

But the managers did not dare make their platform on the issues of the day express their real views. On the contrary, to deceive the West which was largely in sympathy with the South, the Republican platform declared for the "rights of the states to govern their domestic affairs, exclusively, as essential to the perfection and endurance of our political fabric," and as there was then talk of the Southern States seceding, "we denounce the lawless invasion by an armed force, on the soil of any State or Territory no matter under what pretext, as among the gravest of crimes." But evidently, Lincoln was not expected to carry out this party pledge; and he did not.

Mr. Lincoln well understood and himself explained in a speech at Indianapolis what would constitute a commission of "gravest of crimes," when he gave his own definition of the terms "coercion" and "invasion" in declaring "the marching of an army into South Carolina (then having seceded) without the consent of her people would be 'invasion,' and it would be 'coercion' if South Carolinians were forced to submit." But isn't that exactly what he did do within three months after his explanatory approval of the platform upon which he was elected?

However, distrust was so prevalent a million votes were cast against him in the Northern States. Because of four Presidential tickets, three Democratic, Lincoln received only about a third of the popular vote, but a plurality gave him the electoral vote of the Northern States and he

15

was elected. So he could not claim to be acting in response to any popular demand.

His election, however, though by less than a majority even in the Northern States, was regarded in the South as an act of hostility toward the South and the Republican party so intended it; so Southern States began to secede. As to the feeling of bitterness and the intent of the leaders, no man is better qualified to speak than Wendell Phillips, one of the originators and organizers of the Republican party, and he declared that "The Republican party is a sectional party and is organized against the South," and again he made that most remarkable admission: "And I confess we intend to trample underfoot the Constitution of this country."

That is a definition of the "higher law" Seward declared they would appeal to — the setting aside of Constitution, statutes and rights of the states, which was nothing less than mob law by officialdom — culmination of a feeling of bitterness which had been growing for a hundred years and which called forth Washington's order to his army that he would punish severely anyone guilty of revival of "existing sectional animosity." That was in '76 when slavery existed North and South.

In his first Inaugural Address, President Lincoln said, "I have no purpose directly or indirectly to interfere with slavery in states where it exists. I believe I have no lawful right to do so, and I have no inclination to do so." Yet, his acts of war, a month later, were the first steps in that direction, and his Emancipation Proclamation, eighteen months later, another usurpation of power which was in marked contrast to his utterances. He also just as earnestly declared before Congress, to the Southerners, "I will not assail you." But was not that, in view of subsequent events, another "irrepressible conflict" between his promises and his actions?

All authorities having conceded the right to secede, he should not assail. But why try to hold a fort commanding

16

Charleston if coercion was not intended? Which came from his heart — his words or his acts? Was he sincere? Or was he being used by those who secured his nomination? If the latter, where his greatness? It was admitted by the biographer of Cesare Borgia [1476-1507] that "His genius was little more than lack of principle which allowed no scruple to stand in the way of his design." Borgia, too, was idolized by his followers. A cardinal at seventeen, he convulsed his country at thirty, and was killed at thirty-two. He too was listed among the world's great men.

George Lunt, Massachusetts historian, said: "The new President was of scarcely more than ordinary powers — with mind neither cultivated by education or experience — being thus incapable of any wide range of thought or of obtaining any broad grasp of ideas. His thoughts ran in low channels. . . . In his debate with Douglas he said: 'I am not a gentleman and never expect to be.' "

Idolized by some as a great man, Lincoln's utterances from 1847 to 1864 show a most remarkable series of contradictions and inconsistencies. Finally accepting a nomination upon a platform declaring the rights of the states to control their own domestic and internal affairs and against any armed invasion or interference with a seceding state; and by acceptance, pledging himself to that principle and policy, and explaining in a public speech at Indianapolis in February, 1861, his full understanding of this "gravest of crimes," declared against such "gravest crimes," he reiterated such sentiment (if not conviction) in his Inaugural Address, followed by his oath to support the Constitution.

Yet, in a very few weeks after his inauguration he announced his determination to "hold, possess and use the forts of the South to collect customs through Southern ports," which was in itself a practical declaration of war, and, says Hosmer, the historian, "really precipitated the outbreak of an offensive war."

[J. K. Hosmer, author of *Appeal to Arms* and *The Outcome of the Civil War*.]

To attempt to hold the Southern ports and forts by force would be a violation of the Republican platform, Lincoln's frequent avowals of approval, and the Constitutional rights of the states and his oath. He also issued proclamations suspending the writ of habeas corpus, which was also without authority, as Congress alone was vested with that power.

In other words, after Mr. Lincoln became President he seemed to throw off his mask and assume the powers of a despot. Either he had been insincere in his various utterances, or else he owed to the Republican bosses for promotion of his ambition complete subserviency to their stronger will. He was either a puppet in the hands of William H. Seward, Edwin M. Stanton, Lloyd Garrison, Charles Sumner and Thad Stevens, or his greatness was of the Nero brand — power at any price.

[Edwin McMasters Stanton, Secretary of War under Lincoln; appointed to Supreme Court in 1869. . . . William Lloyd Garrison, printer and publisher; president of American Anti-Slavery Society. . . . Charles Sumner, served in U.S. Senate from Massachusetts prior to, during, and in years following the war. . . . Thaddeus Stevens, Congressman from Pennsylvania; leader of radical section of the Republicans in the war years.]

# II

# The Conspiracy to Bring on War

"The secret treachery that caused the war will come to light and justify the South. Truth is deathless." — Admiral Raphael Semmes, Confederate Naval Commander.

In his Inaugural Address, President Lincoln said: "I will not assail you," and later said: "This country with its institutions belongs to the people who inhabit it. Whenever they grow weary of the existing government they can exercise their Constitutional right of amending it, or their revolutionary right to dismember or overthrow it." This, in connection with his declaration that the problem represented an irrepressible conflict, repeated by his Secretary of State, Seward, and the declaration of Secretary of Treasury Chase who, as spokesman for the President at the Peace Conference in Washington, declared that the election of Lincoln was authority to enforce his theories on the country regardless of Constitution, statutes, or decisions of the Supreme Court. These utterances with others of leaders such as W. L. Garrison, Wendell Phillips, John Brown,

Beecher and Chase, show most conclusively that revolution against the Constitution was designed to overthrow the government.

[Henry Ward Beecher, Congregational clergyman, lecturer, author and editor.]

The Confederate States organized their government peacefully — not a gun was fired or a single man injured — when President Lincoln issued orders to Major Anderson, U.S. Commander at Fort Sumter, to "hold the fort," that he was "sending reinforcements." He had refused to consider President Davis' proposal to apportion Federal property (forts, etc.) and the public debt (See *Rec. of Reb.* Vol. 1, p. 109) and now refused to treat with President Davis' commission sent to petition the withdrawal of the troops from Fort Sumter, South Carolina, to avoid an armed conflict.

The Confederate Commissioners, Judge Crawford and John Forsyth, then secured the cooperation of Judges Campbell and Nelson of the Supreme Court, who interceded with President Lincoln and Secretary of State Seward, who finally promised to order the withdrawal of the U.S. troops from Fort Sumter — that the commission could return "assured of finding on their arrival orders to Major Anderson to evacuate Fort Sumter."

[Martin Jenkins Crawford was a Georgia planter and jurist. In addition to his duties as a judge, he served in the Georgia Legislature, and in Congress until the outbreak of the war. Resigning from Congress he served as a delegate to the Provisional Confederate Congress held at Montgomery and was appointed by Jefferson Davis as a member of the peace commission sent by the Confederacy to Washington. When the peace

20

mission failed he became a colonel in the Confederate Army. After the war he resumed his practice as a judge, his final assignment being as an associate justice of the Supreme Court of Georgia. . . . John Archibald Campbell resigned his post as Justice of the Supreme Court in 1862 to become Assistant Secretary of War for the Confederacy. . . . Samuel Nelson, Justice of the Supreme Court.]

Instead, however, the "relief squadron" of eleven vessels, all that time (twenty-three days) being loaded with arms, provisions and two thousand men, arrived off Fort Sumter about the time Commissioners Crawford and Forsyth arrived in Charleston. Upon discovering the base duplicity practiced at Washington and before the fleet could reach Sumter the Confederates, after demanding immediate surrender, reduced the fort and the war was begun. Thus again Lincoln reversed himself.

*Gregg's History of the United States,* pp. 166-67, says: "Suspecting trickery (on report of Lamon's visit to Anderson) Judge Campbell wrote Seward inquiring as to delay, and Seward answered 'Faith as to Sumter fully kept; wait and see.'" At that very moment the secret expedition was started and expected to reach Charleston within forty-eight hours. On the next day after Seward's explicit and written pledge, R. S. Chew, a clerk of Seward's, with a Captain Talbot, appeared in Charleston and, with the eleven-vessel fleet due to arrive the next day, read to Governor Pickens and General Beauregard a paper delivered to Chew by Lincoln on April 6, the day before Seward's last specific pledge to evacuate the fort, notifying the state government that "the Federal government would attempt to supply Sumter with provisions, and if not resisted no attempt would be made to throw in ammunition and men without further notice."

[Francis Wilkinson Pickens was then Governor of South Carolina. Prior to that he had served in Congress and as Minister to Russia. . . . Pierre Gustave Toutant Beauregard graduated from West Point in 1838. He served in the Mexican War with distinction, and as Superintendent of West Point, which position he resigned to become a Confederate general. It was Beauregard who captured Fort Sumter and later was in command at the First Battle of Bull Run.]

This showed an evident purpose to ship in men and ammunition with the supplies and a threat they would eventually do so by force. "That paper by President Lincoln was a declaration of war, and the expedition actual commencement of hostilities, a signal act of treachery," said Gregg.

Again, it is evident that if Lincoln was a good man, sincere and honest in his promises to Judges Campbell and Nelson, then his stronger minds were acting for him, which, to say the least, mixes perfidy or imbecility with greatness, duplicity with statesmanship, until it is difficult to discern where the one begins and the other ends.

When Lincoln became President and Commander in Chief of the Army and Navy of the United States, he, of course, came in possession of information of the treaty or armistice between the United States on the one hand and the Confederate States and the seceding states of South Carolina (December 6, 1860) and Florida (January 29, 1861) on the other hand — both filed in the U.S. War Department and in the U.S. Navy Department — whereby it was solemnly agreed that no attempt would be made by the United States to reinforce Fort Sumter or Fort Pickens, and the Confederate States of America and states would not attack the forts while these solemn agreements were observed. Yet, President Lincoln sent Fox and Lamon into Fort Sumter and Worden to Fort Pickens under guise of friendly messages pertaining to evacuation of the forts, but in fact, as spies, to secure information and convey secret messages.

[Fort Pickens, on Santa Rosa Island at Pensacola, Florida, continued to be occupied by Union forces throughout the war. It is of interest that this fort, now a state park, was later used as a prison where Geronimo and other Apache Indians were confined. . . . Gustavus Vasa Fox was a United States Naval Officer who served in the Mexican War. From 1861 to 1866 he served as Assistant Secretary of the Navy. . . . John Lorimer Worden, Union Admiral, commanded the *Monitor* in her battle with the *Merrimac*.]

To violate an armistice is considered a treacherous act of war. To send a party into such a fort, or any man entering a fort under armistice for the purpose of advising or in any way to reinforce such fort or defense is the act of a spy, is in itself a reinforcement, an act of war. (See *Rec. of Reb.* Vol. I, pp. 111, 114.) For either party to prepare to act against a point covered by armistice is an act of war. This is just another instance of determined disregard for Constitution, law, and humanity.

There were many able men in the North who agreed with Judge Williams, Massachusetts historian, that "The North had no Constitutional right to hold Fort Sumter in case the Southern States seceded, and to hold it meant war." The states gave the land for defense purposes, particularly for defense of the state, and were entitled to their proportion of the Federal property — arsenals, arms and ammunition, as well as forts.

While Northern writers generally say that the war was a result of firing on Fort Sumter, it is a fact fully recorded in the *Records of the "Rebellion"* by Congress that, eleven days before the firing on Fort Sumter, Capt. Israel Vogdes' artillery force, by order of President Lincoln, arrived at Fort Pickens in Florida, instructed by Lincoln to take that fort, and would have done so, but for the refusal of Captain Adams to convey the artillery force to land, Adams urging that such violation of the armistice would bring war. Captain Adams was reprimanded and again commanded to furnish boats to land Captain Vogdes' artillery, which was done on the night of April 11, and the fort taken over by Captain Vogdes, a cause of war, intended to provoke war. But in the greater excitement over Fort Sumter the incident was overlooked. That act of war was prior to the firing of Fort Sumter. (See *Rec. of Reb.* Vol. I, pp. 11-153 and 367, 376.)

After the Fort Sumter incident, President Lincoln called for 75,000 volunteers to invade the South. He could have called Congress to convene, as required by the Constitution, and take that responsibility; but, though he had endorsed the Chicago platform against this "gravest of crimes," he preferred to assume all the responsibility himself. When, however, he did convene Congress on July 4 after he had succeeded by his own unauthorized and despotic acts in irrevocably committing his country to war, and his friends asked Congress to approve of the President's course, Congress declined. This declination is another proof that the country — even the Northern States — (Southern members had all resigned) was up to that time not in accord with the Republican policy which was threatening disunion and war. Then, too, the Joint Resolution presented, but rejected, was admission of the unconstitutionality of his acts.

New York was strongly opposed to that policy and leading public men and newspapers all over the North openly expressed sympathy with the South's position and condition and the *New York Tribune, Express,* and *Herald,* the *Albany Argus* and *Rochester Union* declared the Southern States were justified in seceding to escape the intermeddling and insults which had been hurled at the South. This sentiment was so pronounced, and had been expressed in

24

Lincoln's own state by his defeat for U.S. Senator, that the President could not feel he was acting in response to a public sentiment.

In fact, the *New York Express* on April 15, the day after surrender of Fort Sumter, the day Lincoln called for 75,000 volunteers to invade the South, said, "The people of the United States, it must be borne in mind, petitioned, begged and implored of these men (Lincoln, Seward et al.) who are become their accidental masters, to give them an opportunity to be heard before this unnatural strife was pushed to a bloody extreme, but their petitions were all spurned with contempt; and a conflict begun 'for the sake of humanity' culminates now in inhumanity itself."

Each side blamed the other with being the cause of the war — the one for the first gun, the other for the provocation or necessity. Henry Hallam, a noted English authority on constitutional law, states a universally recognized principle when he said, "The Aggressor in war — that is, he who begins it — is not the first who uses force, but the first who renders force necessary."

As most of the Lincoln propaganda represents the War Between the States as a rebellion on the part of the South without cause, or for slavery solely, I will quote here one from the many I could quote of Northern and Republican leaders: Judge [Benjamin] Williams of Massachusetts said: "There was no need of war. The action of the Southern States was legal and Constitutional, and history will attest that it was reluctantly taken in the last extremity, in the hope of thereby saving their Constitutional rights and liberties from destruction by Northern aggression, which had just culminated in triumph in the Presidential election by the union of North against South — the South was invaded and a war of subjugation was begun by the Federal government."

John A. Logan, afterwards Major General and nominee for Vice-President on the Republican ticket, in the House of Representatives on February 5, 1861, said, "By these

25

denunciations and lawless acts (of Northern people) such results have been produced as to drive the people of the Southern States to a sleepless vigilance for the protection of their property and the preservation of their rights."

The *Albany Argus,* of November 10, 1861, said: "We sympathize with the South. Self-preservation and manhood rightly impelled them to separation from the Union, and we applaud them and wish them God-speed."

The *Rochester Union,* about the same time, said, "Restricting our remarks to actual violations of the Constitution, the North has led the way, and for a long time was the sole aggressor. The South cannot retaliate except by secession."

Judge [Jeremiah] Black, one of the leading jurists of Pennsylvania, said, "They (Northern Republicans) applauded John Brown to the echo for a series of the basest murders on record, and tolled church bells, fired minute guns, and held services in churches draped in mourning, when he was legally hanged. They did not conceal their hostility to Federal and State governments nor deny their enmity to all laws which protected white men. The Constitution stood in their way and they cursed it bitterly. The Bible was quoted against them and they reviled God the Almighty himself." That was the radical minority madness Lincoln represented in his determination to ruin the South, or in his weak subserviency to the masterminds who directed him.

Virginia, the last to secede, before seceding called for a peace conference at Washington, and while a majority west of the Ohio were for peace, the convention was stocked with partisans. For instance, Sen. Zack Chandler of Michigan wired his governor: "Too many peace advocates coming here; send some men with the fighting spirit; unless we can have some bloodletting, this country won't be worth a curse." Evidently Chandler got his "men with the fighting spirit" as the peace advocates were out-generaled.

*Horton's History,* page 62: "Carl Schurz, a notorious

26

agitator and disunionist of Wisconsin, telegraphed from Washington to his governor: 'Appoint some commissioners to Washington conference — myself one — to strengthen our side' " — the faction opposed to any peace measures.

War was on with all its horrors — deaths on the battle-field and deaths in overcrowded prisons. Southern troops captured Federal soldiers faster than they could be cared for — 37,000 were crowded into Andersonville Stockade at one time.

Who suspended the cartel for exchange of prisoners? President Lincoln. President Davis sent one commissioner, and later two, to induce a renewal of the cartel. Lincoln would not permit it, though all the time his own people were clamoring for a renewal of exchange, and he was thereby responsible for a policy which permitted his men to die in Southern prisons, and ours to starve and freeze to death in Northern prisons. He was the cause thereby of thousands of deaths, and untold suffering. He permitted the execution of Southerners contrary to civilized warfare.

It was President Lincoln who issued orders, as Commander in Chief of the Federal Army, to his generals which inaugurated the cruel and inhuman manner of warfare conducted by [Gen. Philip Henry] Sheridan and [Gen. David] Hunter in Virginia and [Gen. William Tecumseh] Sherman on his march-to-the-sea — a war against women, children and old men, pillaging and then burning their homes, after killing all stock and destroying other property they could not carry away. Such war and cruelty were in striking contrast to the war conducted by President Davis and General Lee when Confederate armies were on Northern soil.

When Southern armies went into Pennsylvania and Maryland, President Davis said: "We are not fighting women and children, but men in arms," and these were strict orders: "Private property is not to be injured."

If Lincoln did not plainly order wanton destruction and cruelty, it is a fact that there is no record of his ever

27

disapproving of it. Those orders for devastation did not originate with General Grant. He had no sympathy with such warfare; but as a soldier he passed the order on to his subordinates, and those subordinates are on record as boastfully reporting compliance. It was by "order of the President" that Secretary of War E. M. Stanton issued the order on July 22, 1862 to the commanders of the Federal Army throughout the Southern States to "seize and use any property belonging to the inhabitants," without provision for pay. *(Confederate History Report,* p. 76)

It was also "by order of the President" that a special order was issued to General [John] Pope and General [Adolph Wilhelm Friedrich]Steinwehr [a German Baron], which called forth General Lee's strong protest to the Secretary of War, in which General Lee declared that the Confederate States would be compelled to regard Pope and Steinwehr as "robbers and murderers" not to be treated, if captured, as prisoners of war.

Grant's warfare, his wonderfully kind notes at Appomattox pleading with General Lee to surrender and save thousands of lives and "hundreds of millions of dollars' worth of property not yet destroyed," his magnanimous treatment of Lee on his surrender at Appomattox, and his refusal while President to support illegal and unjust claims of carpetbag governors in the South — all tend to mark Grant as the greatest of the North's leaders of the '60s.

When Lincoln was assassinated great effort was made to place the responsibility on the South. President Davis was charged with complicity, but no proof was ever shown that any Southern man had aught to do with it. It was said that John Wilkes Booth, the assassin, was a bitter Southern sympathizer. He could not have been a very "objectionable partisan" to have been permitted to remain all winter in Washington, with his brother playing every night to full houses of officialdom, including members of the Cabinet and the President himself — and John

28

Wilkes Booth himself a caller on the President. The more plausible story, one seldom heard or printed, is that a friend of Booth was sentenced to be executed, and Lincoln promised Booth a pardon but failed to grant it, and the friend being executed, Booth became so embittered he took the President's life.

[John Wilkes Booth, actor who shot Lincoln on April 14, 1865, was himself shot near Bowling Green, Virginia, twelve days later.]

For one year preceding the Federal President's tragic and lamentable death, his impeachment had been freely discussed by party leaders and predicted. At the election in November, 1864, General McClellan received nearly half the vote, despite the usual doubted wisdom of making change in midst of war, and notwithstanding the President, as Commander in Chief of the Army, used his influence therewith for his reelection. Nearly every member of the Cabinet was at cross-purpose with the President, some of them referring to him disrespectfully as "the fool at the other end of the avenue," and "the idiot in the White House."

[George Brinton McClellan opposed Lincoln on the Democratic ticket.]

But with his death a great change came over the men who must depend for their power upon the future of the party. A few hours after Stanton had spoken in derision of "the idiot in the White House" he stood at the bier of the dead President and pronounced a eulogy upon the "Greatest of Americans," and so did they all begin a systematic acclaim of the greatness of Lincoln — as the only hope of the Republican party.

Had not Lincoln been thus heralded as a martyr, he would have passed into history as a mediocre man with no

29

constructive statesmanship to his credit. But with a war which cost one million lives of his countrymen, and untold suffering to secure what could have been accomplished by real statesmanship without hate, the martyr halo was adopted as essential to the life of the Republican party. Lincoln's death, charged to the South, gave him a fame nothing else would, and the Republican party an influence unequaled in the North and a lease of life fanned by sectional hate.

The statement of some admirers that Lincoln would have been the friend of the South had he lived, is the wildest guess of unthinking men; and I challenge anyone to resurrect an act or utterance, well authenticated, to justify such a statement. Where was his friendship for the South when he broke his pledge to Judges Campbell and Nelson? I have quoted utterances and cited acts of his from 1850 to 1863 to show enmity and vindictiveness toward the South. He certainly had ample opportunity at Hampton Roads and all through the spring of '61 to show even justice for the South.

[As the war neared its final days, a meeting of leaders of the United States and the Confederate States was held on a steamer in Hampton Roads, Virginia. President Lincoln and Secretary of State William H. Seward represented the Union while the Confederacy was represented by Robert M. T. Hunter, J. A. Campbell and Alexander Hamilton Stephens. The meeting produced no results.]

Another self-contradiction: In his inaugural message, Lincoln said to the South, "To you rests the responsibility of war; I will not assail you." He had admitted the right of secession, and now here acknowledged the justice, or at least the legality of the South's position and contention. But to President Davis' commission pleading for withdrawal of the garrison at Fort Sumter, to avoid war, he denied a hearing as he could "not recognize either the seceded states or the Confederacy," and at Hampton Roads he reiterated that position — that he could not admit that the states were out of the Union.

But, upon the Federal occupation of Richmond four years later, he said to representative Virginia Confederates, "You can come back into the Union through the same hole you went out at — by resolution of your convention," thus acknowledging Virginia's position outside the Union.

After saying in his inaugural, "I will not assail you," he spent the next twenty-three days, March 15 to April 9, in organizing four distinct expeditions against Fort Sumter and Fort Pickens — neither commander knowing of the existence of the other, two of these conflicting on the ocean — and one of the Navy Yard commanders (Brooklyn) was instructed "not to inform the Secretary of the Navy." *(Rec. of Reb.* Vol. 1) His manifest purpose was, while publicly deprecating and lamenting the South's exercise of her rights, to conspire secretly and determinedly to provoke or incite war.

Horton (of New York) in his *Causes of the War,* said: "The evening after receipt of the news of the surrender of Fort Sumter to the South Carolinians, Lincoln was particularly cheerful, and gave a reception at the White House, at which he displayed more than his usual vivacity"; and two days later he issued his war proclamation. — *Horton's History,* p. 79.

[Rushman G. Horton, author of *Youth's History of the Great Civil War in the United States from 1861-1865,* published 1868.]

Does not the testimony of history, from even the other side of the line, justify the conclusion that Abraham Lincoln has been greatly misunderstood and overestimated? Doesn't it show that he wanted and maneuvered for war against the South? Not for emancipation of the negro,

31

not for the Union which he had helped to dissolve; but for enmity for the South, and against state sovereignty which allowed the states to control their own domestic affairs and prosper, for hate of wealth and refinement of which he was want to boast antipathy.

As Senator [Stephen A.] Douglas, that able Illinois statesman said, "Lincoln is trying to bring on a cruel war as the surest means of destroying the Union." He certainly did, and by frequent suspensions of the Constitutional rights of the citizen and limitations of the government, he set up a centralized power at Washington which was rapidly approaching dictatorship when his tragic death came.

The one plausible plea of his most devoted admirers is that he "fought to preserve the Union," but that is robbed of its virtue by the fact that he first fought to disrupt the Union, and after disrupting it, admitted with scores of other leading men of his party North, even himself quoting the Republican platform, that the states had the right to secede and the United States had no authority to use coercion against seceding states — that he would "not assail them," and yet — his every act showed that he wanted war. The strongest evidence of the truth of this statement is found in Lincoln's own instruction to General Scott, just before his inauguration as President, about the time he was making that Indianapolis speech defining the Republican platform declaration about coercion and invasion. According to Shepherd's *Life of Lincoln,* he said: "Present my compliments to General Scott, and tell him confidentially to be prepared to hold or retake the forts as the case may require, after my inauguration" — just a few days before his "I will not assail you."

[Winfield Scott, Union general; unsuccessful Whig candidate for President in 1852. . . . Henry Elliott Shepherd of Baltimore, historian and author; served with Confederacy.]

Again, later when Messrs. [Charles H.] Baldwin and Stuart, Union men, from the Virginia Convention [in 1861], then delaying secession, called upon Lincoln to urge delay in action that would force war, Lincoln asked: "What is to become of my revenue in New York if there is ten per cent tariff at Charleston?"

His relief squadrons were then en route and very near Fort Sumter and Fort Pickens.

[Alexander Hugh Holmes Stuart of Virginia served in the Union Congress, as Secretary of the Interior and in the Virginia House of Delegates and State Senate. As a member of the Virginia Convention he did not deny the right of secession, but condemned the move as inexpedient. He took no active part in the war but was a leader in reestablishing peaceful relations when hostilities had ceased.]

Some of the partisan writers claim that Lincoln's relief squadron was not to fire on Fort Sumter or Charleston, but was a ruse to draw the first fire from the Southerners to make them the aggressors. But — if so, his course was just as dishonest and more reprehensible and showed that he did not have the courage to do directly (facing opposition from his own section) what he sought indirectly. The sacrifice of a million lives was no less a "grave crime" by the one than the other method. He accomplished his main purpose by fooling his own people with the cry "The flag has been fired on!" His desire and purpose was war, but he knew that Congress and the Northern people would never sanction it. Hence, his shrewd trick to fool, not the South, but the North — if that claim is correct. But the positive instructions to Major [Harvey] Brown, Lieutenant Scott, Captain Vogdes and Captain Adams at Fort Pickens, and the fact that that expedition did by force take Fort Pickens (*Rec. of Reb.* Vol. I, pp. 361, 376) the

33

night before Sumter was fired on with the entire Navy under orders, does not sustain the claim of merely a "ruse" at Fort Sumter — though his entire secret conspiracy was very clumsy.

Alexander H. Stephens in his *War Between the States* gives Lincoln credit for sincerity in his pledges to Judges Campbell and Nelson that he would order Major Anderson to withdraw from Fort Sumter; but at that time (in 1868) the *Records of the Rebellion,* so-called by Congressional Act, had not been published, and the dozens of orders of President Lincoln organizing the four separate expeditions to Sumter and Fort Pickens were officially unknown to the world outside of the coterie at Washington.

[Alexander Hamilton Stephens, who opposed secession, served as a member of Congress from Georgia from 1843 to 1850 and again from 1873 to 1882. He was elected to the United States Senate in 1866 but was not seated. He was Vice-President of the Confederacy from 1861 to 1865.]

But those records disclose that for all the twenty-three days Judges Campbell and Nelson were pleading with President Lincoln to withdraw the garrison and avoid war, and while the President was repeating every day or two his assurance that the garrison would be withdrawn, he was issuing orders for the preparation of vessels and commissions to Naval officers to get together men, munitions and supplies for the relief expeditions to Fort Sumter and Fort Pickens. There were a dozen or so of such orders bearing Lincoln's signature from March 15 to April 9, only a few of which I will specifically cite:

The conference of the Judges with the President and Secretary of State began on March 15. Judges Campbell and Nelson were assured there was no intention to reinforce Fort Sumter — the garrison would be withdrawn within ten days; but on March 29 Lincoln ordered Secretary of Navy Welles to get three ships at Norfolk Navy Yard ready to go to sea as early as the sixth. (*Rec. of Reb.* Vol. I, pp. 226 and 240) On the thirtieth he ordered Capt. G. V. Fox to go to Brooklyn and prepare transports, naming vessels for an expedition to Fort Sumter. This was followed by several telegrams to Brooklyn and New York Navy yards ordering vessels prepared for Fort Sumter expedition.

[Gideon Welles, editor and Democratic leader; U.S. Secretary of the Navy.]

On March 30, Seward again promised Judges Campbell and Nelson a "satisfactory answer on April 1." On April 1 Seward wrote: "There is no design to reinforce Sumter." On the same date Lincoln ordered vessels and transports ready for expedition to Fort Sumter. (*Rec. of Reb.* Vol. I, p. 229) On the same date Lincoln ordered Lieutenant Scott to report at Brooklyn Navy Yard to Captain Fox, an ex-Navy Officer. On April 1, Lincoln ordered Colonel [Harvey] Brown, then Lieutenant Porter, to proceed to Pensacola, Florida, and "at any cost or risk . . . establish himself in the harbor at Fort Pickens," in spite of the one hundred Confederate guns commanding the entrance.

Judge Campbell called on Seward and showed him a letter he had written President Davis stating Seward's promises with Lincoln's approval whereupon Seward said to Judge Campbell: "By the time that letter reaches its destination Major Anderson will have been ordered to evacuate Fort Sumter." But was that true? On hearing of Colonel Lamon's visit (as spy) to Major Anderson, Judge Campbell, becoming suspicious, again called on Seward and was assured with written memorandum, "Faith as to Sumter fully kept; wait and see."

Then there were other orders of preparation for the four expeditions bearing Lincoln's signature, naming vessels, among them one order for the *Powhatten, Pawnee* and *Harriet Lane,* with three hundred men and twelve months' supplies for four hundred men, for Fort Sumter under Captain Fox. (*Rec. of Reb.* Vol. I, pp. 111-151, 229, 240, 360, 367, 371)

After these negotiations and promises had been progressing from March 15 to April 8, Lincoln sent a special messenger, R. S. Chew, on the ninth with a message to Governor Pickens (Chew reading the notice to Governor Pickens) that he would "supply Fort Sumter with provisions, and if there was no opposition to that he would not further reinforce the fort, *(Gregg's History)* without further notice," which was equivalent to a notice that he would, in accord with another previous declaration, "supply Fort Sumter, peacefully if he could, forcefully if necessary."

When the perfidy was discovered at Montgomery, orders were issued not to await the arrival of the fleet inside, but to demand immediate surrender, and with due regard for human life and every effort to avoid a conflict, if evacuation was still refused, to demolish the fort.

This is not written or uttered in any spirit of animosity or vindictiveness but as an effort to preserve the truth of history. Abraham Lincoln made his own record; and, if he were honest in it, it is presumed that he would today be proud of it, and certainly his admirers are. So, the question then is The Truth. While we are not objecting to the adulation of Lincoln in the North, we do object to certain statements being presented in the South as truth. The truth will not permit his acceptance in the South as a model of statesmanship, when the misrepresentation of his course as Right constitutes a serious reflection on our fathers whom we are sure were guided by principles of Right and Justice.

Neither Davis or Lee, nor one of our statesmen or soldiers of the South ever contended for violation of the Constitution or Federal law; in all the bitter strife the South was not so charged; but the Federal authorities from President down were guilty:

President Lincoln in conspiring to bring on war without the consent of Congress; ordering armed ships to take Forts Sumter and Pickens; his calling for 75,000 volunteers; his suspension of the writ of habeas corpus without authority of Congress; his imprisonment of hundreds of men throughout the North on mere suspicion of sympathy with the South.

[Robert E. Lee, Commanding General of the Confederate States during the last two years of the war; a West Point graduate who served in the Mexican War.]

His Secretary of State (Seward), boasting of this new power to the British Minister at Washington, Lord Lyons, visiting him, said, "I can touch this bell and order the arrest of any prominent man in Ohio and throw him in prison, and I can touch the bell and have thrown in prison a state official of New York, and no power can intervene except the President of the United States. Can the Queen of England do more, my lord?"

Such was the extent of the subversion of the Constitution by the usurpers. It was Salmon P. Chase, Lincoln's spokesman in the peace conference called early in 1861 to try to avoid war, who declared that "the election of Lincoln empowered him and his party to enforce their theories on the country, regardless of the Constitution, the law or rights of the states, or the decisions of the Supreme Court (*Stephens II*, pp. 43-50) and that Lincoln would do so" — and he did.

Five days before Lincoln was inaugurated, Congress passed a resolution pronouncing the theories promulgated by Lincoln and Chase as violative of the Constitution. The Congress just elected, with Lincoln, was known to be even more favorable to the Constitution; and Lincoln, knowing this, would not convene Congress until he had succeeded in inaugurating war.

Lincoln, prompted by the stronger minds of his party managers, perhaps more than by his own will and judgment (for his own will was as varying as the winds), placed his official seal upon proposals and edicts which transformed absolutely in a month or two the sovereignty of the states of the Federation of the founders into a Nation with increased and ever-since-increasing powers in the centralized government at Washington.

Benjamin T. Wade, U.S. Senator from Ohio, and prominent in several Republican administrations, said in 1861: "Who is to be the final arbiter (as to secession) — the Federal Government or the State? Why, to yield the right of the State to protect its own citizens, would consolidate this government into a miserable despotism." This is just what was done by President Lincoln's despotic overthrow of the Constitution, a fundamental and sacred law which had been respected and revered for a hundred years.

The *Washington Post* of August 14, 1906, said: "Let us be frank about it. The day the people of the North responded to Abraham Lincoln's call for troops to coerce the Sovereign States, that day the Republic died, and the Nation was born."

Now, after viewing Mr. Lincoln's acts from the several angles, one is prompted to ask, "Why did he cause the war?" Recalling his expressed conflicting opinions on the slavery question; his influence against the Crittenden Compromise, urging the Republicans to defeat it; the violent speech of Chase, his spokesman in the Peace Conference, and his opposition to several other peace overtures including the two special commissions from Pres. Jefferson Davis — the idea that he "yearned for peace" falls flat.

[Crittenden Compromise, a measure urged in the United States Senate by John J. Crittenden, 1860-1861, providing establishment of the slave line of 36° 30' N., and for the enforcing of the fugitive-slave laws.]

When his own people of the Northern States were so strongly opposed to his policy that he dared not submit the issues to Congress, or (as petitioned) to a vote of the Northern States, his friends cannot claim that he was acting in response to a public demand. Abolitionists supposed, and the negroes were taught, that freedom of the negro was the controlling motive; but this view is contradicted by declarations that he had no power under the Constitution to free them, and "certainly had no desire to do so," and later "if he could preserve the Union by perpetuating slavery he would do so." How could he claim "preservation of the Union" as his motive when his own bitter campaign and the animosity and hostility therein engendered was the main cause of the dissolution of the Union?

The Crittenden resolutions could have preserved the Union; the Peace Conference was designed to do so; recognition and negotiation with President Davis' commission to avoid collision at Fort Sumter might have restored the Union — at least would have preserved the peace Lincoln claimed his soul was "yearning for"; even the commission which met him and Seward at Hampton Roads in 1864 could have restored peace and probably the Union had he treated with them. But all these efforts he strenuously opposed and his followers fought. So, what could have been the incentive, the prime motive which actuated him in forcing the war — unless it was his own inborn hostility to the South and Southern people?

We repeat, we entertain no bitterness for the Federal soldier, and naught but respect for their descendants, but we do insist upon believing in the virtue, the wisdom and the patriotism of our fathers who contended ably and valiantly fought for the preservation of the principles of states' sovereignty won from England in '76 and by the

39

Revolutionary fathers established in our Constitution — principles they believed right, knew were right, were right.

To those Southerners (if there be any) who would apologize for the part of the South in the war, I will quote from Mr. Davis himself: "Let none of the survivors of these men offer in their behalf the penitential plea that they 'believed' they were right. Be it ours to transmit to posterity our unequivocal confidence in the righteousness of the cause for which these men died."

# III

# Contrast with the Administration
# of
# Jefferson Davis

But this was to be a discussion of both Davis and Lincoln, the two Presidents of the war period of the '60s, so we will revert to the Confederate President.

Jefferson Davis was respected and revered as a knightly gentleman and gallant soldier, an able statesman, a courageous and uncompromising defender of the Constitution, contending for the preservation of the Union while others were lighting the fires of destruction, a wise and unselfish organizer and administrator of the Confederacy; and yet at its fall he patiently and heroically bore the brunt of the hate for the South, suffering in prison cell and shackles, the victim of concentrated partisan animosity.

Jefferson Davis contributed more and suffered more than any other man for the cause whose heroes we now honor and revere. When Richmond fell it was upon Jefferson Davis the full force of Northern vengeance fell. Why?

41

Because, as I have said, President Davis was the trusted leader, the guiding hand of the Confederacy, contributing most to its structure, and by his able statesmanship as President and generalship as Commander in Chief of the army, almost winning victory in the first two years of the war.

[Jefferson Davis, in addition to his duties as President, served the Confederacy as Commander in Chief of the army for the first two years. He was succeeded in that position by Robert E. Lee.]

Jefferson Davis was the son of Samuel Davis, a hero of the Revolution. He was born in Kentucky in 1808, and soon after, with his father, moved to Mississippi, which was his home the greater part of his eventful life. After having received an academic education, he went to Transylvania College in Kentucky, and while closing a successful term there was appointed by President Monroe to a cadetship in West Point Military Academy. There he also won high honors, graduating in 1828 at the age of twenty years.

For seven years he served in the United States Army as a lieutenant, and for distinguished bravery in the Black Hawk War he was commissioned First Lieutenant of Dragoons in 1835. Soon thereafter he resigned his commission and returned to Mississippi to enjoy life on his plantation. However, the people of his district, recognizing his abilities, manifested their sound judgment in electing him to Congress, where he became prominent as a participant in all debates upon the great questions of the day. He became especially interested in the pending trouble with Mexico, and resigned his seat in Congress to enter the army as a defender of his country. Few have been the instances, indeed, when patriotism is manifested by a man resigning a seat in Congress to enter the fighting ranks. But that was Jefferson Davis.

He fought through the Mexican War, displaying marked gallantry at the Battle of Monterrey. Just here I recall when Gen. Zachary Taylor came to acknowledge his merit and pay him honor. Davis had married General Taylor's daughter, under parental objection, the General saying to his daughter that "Jeff was only a soldier." But after the Battle of Buena Vista, where Colonel Davis saved the day for the Americans, the General sent for Davis and, taking him by the hand, said, "I have concluded that my daughter was a better judge of men than I."

It was at the Battle of Buena Vista where Colonel Davis a second time distinguished himself and, though wounded and attacked by a superior force of 5,000 regulars, and for a long time unprotected, he formed his regiment into the form of a V, maintained his ground and repelled for the last time the hosts of Mexico. Thus upon the field of battle, Jefferson Davis proved that he was not only a scholar and a statesman, not a mere pampered son of wealth, but a soldier and a successful defender of his country's flag.

His V formation and manner of heroic attack against overwhelming numbers was adopted by Colin Campbell in India and applauded in England. For Colonel Davis' bravery and successful conduct of his part of the campaign against Mexico, President Polk tendered him a commission as brigadier general, but Colonel Davis declined the honor upon the ground that the President was not authorized by the Constitution to make the appointment.

[Colin Campbell, British field marshal; elevated to the peerage as Baron Clyde of Clydesdale in 1858.]

Here again we have the consistent and unselfish adherence to the Constitution. Though the President's appointment was confirmed by both Houses of Congress, Colonel Davis again refused to accept an honor which he contended was unauthorized by the Federal Constitution, that right

43

and authority being invested with the state. There was no question of slavery in this, but it was the same strict interpretation of the Constitution which led him to leadership in opposition to the marked disregard for that fundamental law by the Northern representatives and members of the Federal government in the years immediately preceding and following Lincoln's election.

In 1852 Colonel Davis was called to President Pierce's Cabinet as Secretary of War, where he displayed great constructive statesmanship. While in that position he laid the foundation for the Smithsonian Institution, established new posts on the frontier, planned trade routes across the western territories to the Pacific, and was the first to propose a transcontinental railway connecting the Atlantic and Pacific, contributing greatly to the development of the West, had extensions made to the Capitol Building, and marked improvements in army accouterments and ammunitions. For an improvement in a revolver, Colt's Armory made and presented him with a very handsome revolver with the improvement and suitably engraved "To a brother inventor."

He was the first to suggest camels for transportation of military supplies through the barren West, where he strengthened forts difficult to reach, and was first to suggest the purchase of the Panama Canal Zone. He planned closer relations with China and Japan and South Africa. He proposed and was responsible for the new Senate Hall and the House of Representatives. He sent George B. McClellan to the Crimea to study British and Russian military tactics; he appointed Robert E. Lee superintendent of West Point, and advanced Albert Sidney Johnston to important posts.

[Albert Sidney Johnston graduated from West Point in 1826 and resigned his commission eight years later. He enlisted in the Army of the Republic of Texas as a private and rose to the rank of

Commander in Chief. He reentered the United States Army in 1849, and commanded an expedition to Utah in 1857. When the Confederacy was formed he resigned his commission as brigadier general and became a full general in the Confederate Army. His death at Shiloh resulted in the loss of the battle by the Confederates.]

Davis was nominated for President by Massachusetts men in 1860, but refused to permit his name to be presented to the Charleston convention. He stood consistently and firmly for what Lincoln preached but did not practice — not to overthrow the Constitution, but to overthrow the men who perverted the Constitution. When Mr. Davis, as Secretary of War, was contending for an increase in the army for defense of the West, other leaders were calling it a desert unfit for human habitation. The people of every state west of the Mississippi River should honor Jefferson Davis for the great service he rendered them both in war and in peace during the formative period of their history.

He was twice elected United States Senator, and his services were characterized by great ability, courage and fidelity to the Constitution; and as disregard for that instrument marked the course of Senators and others high in government, his warning voice was to be heard: "Strict interpretation and obedience to the mandates of that fundamental law must be the price of Union and stability of the government."

The unfortunate division of the Democratic party in 1860 with two electoral tickets in the field dividing the vote, and even a fourth at the general election, allowed Lincoln to win the Presidency on a minority of the popular vote, though securing the electoral vote of the Northern States. That partisan vote in the North, together with the bitterness which characterized Lincoln's campaign, indicated to the South the hostility which might be expected from the incoming administration.

Then came talk of secession, the withdrawing from the Union of the Southern States. While leaders of the new Republican party boldly declared their hostility to the South, Jefferson Davis, then in the Senate his second term, loved the Union and frequently so expressed himself. To Judge Campbell with whom he had served in President Pierce's Cabinet, he said: "I love the old Union; my father died for it; but unless you have been in the South, you cannot begin to estimate the bitterness already engendered by partisanship in the North." He so strongly adhered to the Union, preferring to contend there for their rights, that some of the Southern leaders had ceased to confer with him upon the turbulent issues.

In his frequent debates upon the issues of the day, he expressed hope that peaceful means would prevail, and that all differences would be adjusted inside the Union. But his counsels could not prevail against such aggressiveness and bitter enmity for the South as was reflected by Sen. Zack Chandler of Michigan in his telegram to his Governor on assembling of the Peace Conference, asking him to "Send some men down here with the fighting spirit; there is decidedly too much peace talk. Without a little blood-letting this Union will not, in my opinion, be worth a curse."

Judge George L. Christian of Richmond, Virginia, in a very able paper on the *Cause of the War and the Aggressor,* says: "The Southern States had not only the right to secede, but just cause for withdrawing from the Federation; and in the exercise of that right were forced to fight in defense of home and country"; and asks, "Why should not our children and their children know the truth?"

The view of this representative Southerner is also the view of many of the leading men of the North. Dozens of editorials of Northern newspapers could be quoted, but I will quote only one here: The *Albany* (New York) *Argus* said: "We sympathize with and justify the South; their rights have been invaded, Constitution disregarded, their

46

feelings insulted, interests and honor assailed — and if we deemed it certain that the animus of the Republicans could be carried into the Federal administration, all instincts of self-respect and manhood would impel them to separation from the Union, and we would applaud and wish them Godspeed." Similar views were expressed by other New York and Eastern papers, and by Judge Jeremiah Black of Pennsylvania, Judge [Benjamin J.] Williams, noted writer of Massachusetts, Josiah Quincy, Horace Greeley, and Gen. Don Piatt, and we might add Abraham Lincoln, if that counts.

[Don Piatt, author, journalist and jurist; founder of the *Washington Capitol;* served in Union Army.]

Mr. Davis wrote to ex-President Pierce on January 20, 1861: "Those who have driven the states to secession threatened to deprive them of the right to require that their government shall rest upon the consent of the governed, to substitute foreign force for domestic support, to reduce the state to the condition from which the colonies rose," through revolution against foreign power.

In Senator Davis' famous address to the Senate January 21, 1861 (the day after writing the letter to Pierce), bidding farewell to the members with whom he had so long served, in closing an able presentation of the position and grievances of the South, differences in interpretation of the Constitution of the Fathers of the Republic, he said: "Then, Senators, we recur to the compact which binds us together; we recur to the principles upon which our government was founded, and when you deny them, and when you deny us the right to withdraw from a government which, thus subverted, threatens to be the destruction of our rights, we but tread the path of our fathers when we proclaim our independence and take the hazard. This is done, not in hostility to others, not to injure any section of the country, not even for our own pecuniary benefit, but for the high and solemn motive of defending and protecting the rights we inherited, and which it is our duty to transmit unshorn to our children."

Then again, he showed the calm dispassionate spirit of the Christian statesman when he said: "In the course of my service here, I see around me some with whom I have served long. There may have been points of collision, but whatever there has been of offense to me, I leave here; I carry with me no hostile remembrance. Whatever of offense I have given, which has not been redressed, or for which satisfaction has not been demanded, I have, Senators, in this hour of parting, to offer my apology for any pain which in the heat of discussion, I have inflicted. I go hence unencumbered of the remembrance of any injury received and having discharged the duty of making the only reparation in my power for any injury offered."

He thus left the Senate with a heavy heart although pursuing the course which his conscience dictated to him was demanded.

Imbued with the doctrine of States' Rights, the sovereignty of the states which was reserved when the Constitution was framed; the endorsement of this principle by nearly every man North or South, supported by the fact that all the New England States at Concord in 1814 had threatened to exercise that right of withdrawal from the Union — he felt that he was exercising a clear right, though painful, in resigning to follow his state which had voted secession. So, with sorrowing heart he followed Conviction and Right.

By the time Mr. Davis reached Mississippi, his state, recognizing his great military ability, as displayed in the Black Hawk and Mexican wars, had already elected him Commanding General and authorized him to organize the State Militia, and while engaged in that task the Confederate Convention at Montgomery elected him President of the Confederate States. He entered upon that supreme

48

responsibility and from chaos soon had perfected a complete government for the new republic of the Confederate States of America.

[The Confederate Convention met at Montgomery, Alabama on February 4, 1861, and formed a provisional government.]

President Davis was for peace. The Confederate government was organized without any incident of unpeaceful nature, a Constitution was adopted, a section declaring against the importation of slaves; not a gun was fired; and there would have been no war, had not Lincoln's government forced it by his unconstitutional and belligerent attitude as to Fort Sumter.

To the Confederate commission sent to Washington by President Davis to beseech the Washington government, in the interest of peace, to withdraw the United States garrison from Fort Sumter, which was in South Carolina territory, President Lincoln for twenty-three days promised it would be done; and yet instead of ordering Major Anderson to withdraw from Fort Sumter (See Lincoln's orders in *Rec. of Reb.* Vol. I, pp. 120-376), he ordered him to hold the fort, that a fleet of war vessels with reinforcements was en route, President Lincoln having previously announced that he would hold the Southern forts and collect tax on imports through the ports of the South.

Jefferson Davis, on April 7, while awaiting the result of his commission to Washington proposing to President Lincoln a peaceful adjustment of differences, a division of forts and other properties, and an apportionment of the public debt, that would avoid war, said: "With the Lincoln administration rests the responsibility of precipitating a collision and the fearful evils of a cruel war."

Having exhausted every effort to prevent war, when news came that the armed fleet with reinforcements was en route, and just before they would have arrived in South

49

Carolina waters, and after President Lincoln's special messenger (Chew) handed Governor Pickens a written notice that he would reinforce the fort, President Davis authorized a demand for the immediate surrender of the fort. Upon Anderson's refusal, Secretary of War Leroy P. Walker of the Confederacy ordered General Beauregard, who was in charge of an improvised force of volunteer South Carolinians, to demand immediate evacuation of the fort, and, on refusal, fire on the fort and reduce it. How promptly and effectually that order was obeyed is a matter of history. And the fact remains, also, that it was the threatened invasion by an armed enemy fleet which called for the order. The fleet got within sight or hearing of Fort Sumter and after the battle turned about and returned. Major Anderson was permitted to return North with his troops.

Almost simultaneously with the sending of the armed fleet came the destruction of the fort at Harpers Ferry in Virginia by the retiring U.S. troops, and the burning of shipping and destroying of the garrison at Norfolk, Virginia, as U.S. troops abandoned that place. Thus was the war begun, as had been planned, no doubt, by the Zack Chandlers, Thad Stevenses, Sumners, Sewards and Lincoln — a direct result of the election of President Lincoln.

Northern writers usually state that "the shot at Fort Sumter was the first gun of the war." But, in fact, the first gun of the war was the one placed on the transport by order of President Lincoln bound for Fort Sumter; but the "shot which was heard round the world" was the one fired at Fort Sumter in home defense. Going back a year, it might be said that the first gun of the war was the one (or score) furnished by Henry Ward Beecher for John Brown's proposed insurrectionary raid into Virginia, and referred to by Northern papers as "Beecher's Bibles."

President Davis has been criticized for many things, unjustly as investigation would prove. For instance, he has been criticized for "not accepting the proposal of President Lincoln for ending the war," and it has even been stated

50

by these uninformed critics that President Lincoln proposed to "concede the slaves if the South would come back into the Union," and that "Lincoln proposed to pay $400,000,000 for the slaves, and Davis refused."

That is all without any foundation. Governor Lubbock [of Texas], who was at the time on President Davis' personal staff, conversed with Vice-President Stephens, R. M. T. Hunter and Judge Campbell, the commissioners sent by President Davis to meet President Lincoln and his Secretary of State on their vessel in Hampton Roads off Fortress Monroe, and those gentlemen said, and in their reports to President Davis reported, that no proposal of any terms was submitted by either side; but that the main result of the conference was that "President Lincoln gave them to understand that he could not treat with the Confederate States."

Alexander H. Stephens, in his *War Between the States* Vol. II, also says Lincoln stated he could not make any treaty or agreement with the representatives of the states separately, as that would be a recognition of their separate government, and that he would only accept their "unconditional surrender" and treat with them "after they had returned into the Union" — which, in effect, would have been for the Southerners to have acknowledged themselves and the states to be "rebels" with whatever penalties the victors might see fit to inflict, which they could not at all consider.

President Lincoln's own report to Congress says: "No terms were submitted by either side." Lubbock, in his memoirs, from which I get his version, says that by fighting on, the South obtained in the surrender of Lee to Grant far better terms and fairer recognition than could have been had from Lincoln.

Judge John H. Reagan also published a full statement in accord with these facts, in which he said: "These reports have been repeated by some citizens of acknowledged ability and repute, who believed them, but in them there was no truth." The purpose of the originators was "to raise Lincoln and lower Davis in the public estimation, by showing that President Davis could have secured acceptable terms and $400,000,000 in payment for slaves; but," Judge Reagan says, "the report of the commissioners sent to Hampton Roads by President Davis signed by Messrs. Stephens, Hunter and Campbell, reported to the contrary, and states that no terms at all were proposed by Lincoln, and that no terms could have been considered except by unconditional surrender."

[John Henniger Reagan was a member of Congress from Texas prior to the war and following the war, later serving in the U.S. Senate. During the war he was Postmaster General of the Confederacy.]

Judge Reagan says that the only suggestion of compensation he ever heard of as coming from Lincoln was that the border states provide for emancipation with compensation (this was a year prior to Lincoln's Proclamation of Emancipation exempting the border states from its operation), which was not accepted by the border states as it was evidently made to defeat the seceding states, and there was no assurance that it would have been approved by the North — or by Lincoln.

[The "border states," where loyalty was divided, were Delaware, Maryland, Kentucky and Missouri.]

However, this had no connection with the Hampton Roads conference. George Lunt, another Massachusetts historian, says of the much talked of $400,000,000 slave compensation: "Lincoln's plan was to free the slaves in the South by war, and pay $400,000,000 by Congressional act to Northern slaveholders," probably meaning Dela-

52

ware, the border states, and Illinois where General Grant's slaves were.

Ben Hill of Georgia, member of the Confederate Senate and confidential friend of President Davis, said: "You have heard it said that the President embarrassed the commissioners by giving them positive instructions to make the recognition of independence an ultimatum, a condition precedent to any negotiations. That is not true. I have it from Mr. Davis' own lips that he gave the commissioners no written instructions and no ultimatum. He gave them, in conversation, his views, but leaving much to their discretion saying: 'They could best judge how to conduct the conference when they met.' His own opinion was, that it would be most proper and wise so to conduct it, if they could, as to receive rather than make propositions. While he did not feel authorized to yield our independence in advance, and should not do so, though he would not deceive Mr. Lincoln, it might be well for them to secure an armistice, although Mr. Lincoln might understand that reunion must, as a result, follow. However, he had little hope of success, after he learned that Seward and Lincoln would both be there."

All other authorities that I have read deny the report that Lincoln said, "Keep your slaves and come back into the Union" or anything like it. But, supposing he had made such a proposition, it would not have been accepted, for the South was contending for a principle far greater than the moneyed value of slaves, which was merely an incidental issue, the excuse of the Northern partisans.

President Davis occupied a most trying position at the head of the new government. Though his success in organizing it had been marked, there grew up differences of opinion as to this policy or that appointment in the army; and there are some who blame the President for much of the failure. But no man could have accomplished more; no man could have guided the Confederacy to victory against such fearful odds in men and resources. It is a matter of congratulation that the Southern Army won almost every battle for the first two years, with odds of three-to-one against the South when our ports were blockaded and supplies cut off, and the odds were increased by importations for the Northern Army from Europe, to nearly six-to-one, the official figures showing the total of all enlistment to be 2,870,000 to 643,000 with the greater difference the last two years.

In view of this record it can be truly said that Jefferson Davis' administration was a great success though our armies were so overwhelmingly outnumbered. Our forces under Lee, Jackson, the Johnstons, and associates fought bravely and unfalteringly, while the Northern armies were worn out and their commanders frequently changed because of their defeat.

> [Thomas Jonathan (Stonewall) Jackson was a West Point graduate and served in the Mexican War. He won the sobriquet "Stonewall" for his stubborn stand at the first Battle of Bull Run. He was killed, through an error, by his own men at the Battle of Chancellorsville on May 2, 1863. . . . Joseph E. Johnston, not to be confused with Albert Sidney Johnston, was also a West Point graduate and veteran of the Mexican War. He surrendered to Sherman at Durham Station, North Carolina on April 26, 1865, seventeen days after Lee's surrender.]

The Confederates captured Federals faster than the South could prepare prisons for them. By the way, it would not be amiss just here to say that the Confederates killed, wounded, and captured a man-and-a-half for every man enlisted in the Southern Army; while the casualties in the Confederate Army were less than a quarter-of-a-man to each Federal soldier. Doesn't that speak volumes for the bravery and efficiency of the army under Jefferson Davis? It was the greatest military achievement of the age.

54

# IV

# Slavery – Not the Cause of the War

It has been so often said that slavery was the cause of the War Between the States, but I would suggest it could not have been. A generous and enlightened people could not have introduced slavery and, having sold their own, inaugurate a cruel war to liberate the slaves of their neighbors rather than by compensation.

The *Desire* of Massachusetts was the first American ship to engage in kidnapping Africans and selling them in America; Massachusetts was the first state to establish perpetual slavery by law. (See *Mass. Hist. Col.*, Vol. 8, p. 231.) Massachusetts was the first to enact a Fugitive Slave Law; and the last state to legislate against slavery was Massachusetts. Fifty years after the Federal government had (on motion of a Southern man) prohibited importation of slaves, the *Nightingale* of Massachusetts was, in 1861, en route to America when captured with nine hundred Africans in her hold, captured by Captain Guthrie nine days after the surrender of Fort Sumter. The *Cradle of Liberty* of Boston and Girard College in Philadelphia were both built by money made in the slave traffic. This is just to keep the record straight; no Southern man or ship ever engaged in slave traffic.

The South had been for many years discussing the abolition of slavery and one measure in the Virginia Assembly was finally lost on a tie vote. The first colony to forbid slaves was Georgia, and the first state to legislate against the slave trade was Georgia; the only state to make it a felony to buy a slave was Virginia. Many of our leading statesmen were desirous of abolishing the institution brought South by New England, and which was supported by the traffic of New England ships, but the serious problem was "What shall we do with them?" It was never suggested to sell them, as New England sold them to the South, or to dump them into the jungles of Africa.

Several Southern slaveholders, among them John Randolph, through Bishop Meade, manumitted their slaves, settling them in comfortable homes in Ohio where the town of Xenia now stands, but white men from the East took their lands away from them.

[John Randolph served intermittently in the Senate from 1799 to 1834 and as Minister to Russia. . . . The Reverend William Meade, Episcopal Bishop, served his church in Virginia until his death in 1862.]

Just here let me say that General Lee declared that "no just man could defend the institution of slavery." He freed his slaves at the beginning of the war. Gen. Joseph E. Johnston and Gen. Albert Sidney Johnston owned no slaves; Stonewall Jackson owned none and believed they should be free; Dr. Hunter McGuire, a noted authority, says he knew nearly every man in Stonewall Jackson's army and not one in thirty was a slave owner. My father was a newspaper publisher, owned no slaves, but advocated secession because of the wrongs of the North, and was captain of one of the first companies going into action.

56

War for slavery! It is one of the calumnies against the South. But General Grant kept his slaves at work even after Lincoln's Emancipation Proclamation, and until the adoption of the Thirteenth Amendment to the Constitution, during Reconstruction.

Just here, it is not amiss to say that inasmuch as President Lincoln's Emancipation Proclamation exempted from its operation the states of Delaware, Maryland, Kentucky and Missouri, where he supposedly had authority, and was operative only in the seceded states where he had none, it must have been a hypocritical play for Northern or European consumption, or else was designed to encourage the negroes to revolt and insurrection and massacre, after the manner of John Brown's plan. He certainly did not believe his proclamation would emancipate the negro in the South. No such illogical or inconsistent act ever spotted Jefferson Davis' official conduct.

It is with much reluctance I again here have to refer to Lincoln's conduct or course of action. But it is an instance where both could not be right. It is equally clear that one was the aggressor in a great war of invasion and conquest; the other a contender for the Union under the Constitution and a leader in a war of defense of home and country.

If President Davis thought he could have prevented the war, he was wrong; he sent a commission to plead with Lincoln to withdraw Anderson from Fort Sumter and avoid war. If he could have stopped it and did not try, he was wrong; he sent a commission to Hampton Roads asking for an armistice and peace, which Lincoln refused to consider. If he could have prevented the heavy mortality in prisons North and South and failed to try, he was wrong; but he hastened exchanges until stopped by Lincoln, and thrice renewed efforts to renew the cartel for exchange, which Lincoln's orders prevented. These are mere truths of history that should be preserved.

Again, President Davis was criticized for certain changes

in military commanders. He may have erred in some of the few changes, but no man has ever said that he was actuated by any but the purest patriotic motives, and the best interests of the Confederacy. What man could have steered a government so new, and hastily organized an army without friction or mistake? Lincoln made more changes in the Federal Army than President Davis did in the Confederate Army and yet his forces won, but it was not due to his wisdom so much as to the resources which enabled him to supply men as fast as the South killed and captured them.

It was said of Grant (how true I cannot say) that he would wire Lincoln: "Send me another army — they have killed and captured this one." It was beyond the power of man to cope longer than two years against odds which increased from three-to-one at the beginning of the war to six-to-one at its close, with proportionate increased advantage in resources. But in estimating President Davis' abilities as President and Commander in Chief of the army (he was Commander in Chief the first two years), let us remember that for the first two years the Confederate forces as organized and conducted by him won almost every battle; and had really won two great battles which were lost by the tragic deaths of the commanders — Stonewall Jackson at Chancellorsville, accidentally killed by his own men, and Albert Sidney Johnston at Shiloh — where in both instances the deaths of the commanders were such a shock to the men that, amid grief and confusion, time was lost until reinforcements came to the vanquished Federals and turned our victory into defeat.

What would have been the result and effect on the war had Grant's Army remained captured at Shiloh, and Hooker's at Chancellorsville? No man can say. Chickamauga was a signal victory by the Confederates and would have been followed by another at Missionary Ridge but for shortage in ammunition. General Bragg found he had not enough ammunition to hold the Ridge, so was forced to retire as best he could, and even that was with the loss of 5,000 or 6,000 prisoners, among whom was my father's entire company. Yes, President Davis was an able executive and successful commander of the army, and true to his people and their cause. What commander could have won against the hordes of Europe?

[Gilbert here refers to the large number of mercenaries from Europe who fought with the Union Army.]

Jefferson Davis' armies were twice very near the gates of Washington. The first great victory of Manassas and the utter rout of the Union forces and their ignominious flight to Washington pell-mell with the official and society leaders who had "gone to see the rebels whipped" was the great comedy of the war. Then, there's the tragedy of Gettysburg, where both armies were exhausted, worn out against each other. Pickett's immortal charge left an impress they never knew.

[George Edward Pickett, West Point graduate and veteran of the Mexican War, was a Confederate general.]

General Lee, appalled at the loss of human life, and General Meade, viewing the even greater slaughter of his own men, both prepared to withdraw from the scene of carnage. From Meade's high point of observation was noted a retiring movement on the part of Lee. Meade stopped, watched and waited, and to him was accorded the victory. Had Lee held out another half hour victory would have perched on the banner of the Confederacy, and — on to Washington. The number engaged was about 100,000 Union and 65,000 Confederates. Jefferson Davis was Commander in Chief of the 65,000 Grays, which met the 100,000 Blues at Gettysburg.

[George Gordon Meade, Union General, also
was a graduate of West Point and a Mexican War
veteran.]

Another misrepresentation of President Davis, the gross-
est and most outrageously false, was, coming from the
enemy of course, a direct responsibility for the heavy
mortality in Andersonville prison in southern Georgia. I
recently visited the place; there were altogether during the
war more than 53,000 prisoners confined there, 32,000 at
one time. Of course it was impossible to provide sanitary
regulations in a camp of that magnitude, and almost as
difficult to provide them with wholesome food and the
kind they had been used to. The result was sickness and
epidemic during the hot months when the death rate
reached as high as fifty to sixty a day — a total of 13,700
during the war.

The North, overlooking the fact that the Southern
soldier fared even worse in Northern prisons, made great
complaint against the management of Andersonville prison,
and a few months after the close of the war, Maj. Henry
Wirz, the commander of the prison, was arraigned on a
charge of murder, and while the Federal government had
the South by the throat under military rule, Major Wirz
was condemned by court-martial and hanged. Federal authorities offered him freedom and life if he would give
testimony which would implicate President Davis in a
plan for maltreatment of prisoners. This proposal was in-
dignantly spurned by Major Wirz, and the imputation
denounced as false without any foundation.

The fact that conditions were so bad in Andersonville
prison, while most regrettable, is nevertheless creditable
to the skill and valor of the Confederates, for our boys in
gray captured the boys in blue faster than we could provide
for their accommodation.

Recalling the fearful accusation of bitter partisans of
responsibility of President Davis for the unusual mortali-

ty among Andersonville prisoners, we can only refer to written history which abundantly records that after President Lincoln suspended the cartel for the exchange of prisoners and President Davis had twice endeavored to renew the cartel, he said to the Federal government that "they had made drugs and medicines contraband of war, the first time in the history of civilized nations," but that he would exchange the North cotton for drugs to be used in Andersonville prison; and that being refused, he proposed that the Federal government send down its own physicians and medicines under Confederate guarantee of safe conduct and every courtesy, and that was refused. And yet they maligned President Davis and hanged Wirz.

The Southern people erected a very imposing monument to the memory of Major Wirz just outside the old stockade which has been made a national cemetery by the Federal government, and upon this monument engraved in the marble base is a quotation from General Grant, evidently an apology to the Northern clamor for exchange of prisoners, which is in substance as follows, as near as I can recall the words: "Liberation of our soldiers from Southern prisons would be a most humanitarian thing, but if we should exchange prisoners now, it would result in the defeat of Sherman's army." Certainly an awful admission, that three of their men released could not be equal in fighting force to two Southern released prisoners.

[That portion of the wording on the monument credited to Grant literally reads: "It is hard on our men held in Southern prisons not to exchange them, but it is humanity to those left in the ranks to fight our battles. At this particular time to release all prisoners North would insure Sherman's defeat and would compromise our safety here. — Ulysses S. Grant. Aug. 18, 1864."]

After the execution of Major Wirz, Sen. Ben Hill made

61

thorough investigation of the records, procured the number of prisoners confined in each prison of the North and of the South, and the number of deaths in each, and had it embodied through a speech in the Senate in the Congressional Record, showing that while the South had 270,-000 Federals in Southern prisons, and the North had only 220,000 Confederates in her prisons, there were 26,326 deaths in the Northern prisons and only 22,756 deaths in the Southern prisons — 50,000 more men in Southern than in Northern prisons, but 3,570 more deaths in the North. And yet they blamed Jefferson Davis and hanged Wirz, while the death record was twelve percent in Northern, as against nine percent in Southern prisons.

# V

# Davis Taken Prisoner

With Richmond almost completely surrounded, President Davis deemed it wise to move the seat of government farther south, for he was not yet without hope of success. Gen. Joe Johnston was still fighting, and there were the Army of the Tennessee and the Western armies winning occasional victories. So the President and his Cabinet moved on south, to Greensboro, and thence into Georgia. Hearing of Johnston's surrender, they concluded to make their way to west of the Mississippi where, with Gen. Kirby Smith, it was still hoped to prolong the war to success.

The Federals, however, did not intend to let the President escape. At Irvington, Georgia, the President's party went into camp, as it developed, for the last time. Next morning, May 10, 1865, while it was slowly raining, horses were gotten ready for the start west, when suddenly the Federals were all about them and coming from opposite directions, firing at each other. Governor Lubbock, in his memoirs, said that President Davis was dressed in the clothes he usually wore, sitting on a log, a light rain cloak thrown around his shoulders, when he was arrested. Governor Lubbock called to the Federal commander to stop firing and killing each other.

He says that the story of the President endeavoring to escape in female attire was contemptibly false, as everyone there knew. "His conduct was that of a brave soldier and his bearing such as might have been expected from a man who had often met perils unmoved — a great general whose sun was sinking below the horizon after stormy days of battle, of a noble spirit capable of dying, if fortune so willed, upon the block without the tremor of a muscle, without blanching of the cheek by the absence of a single wonted crimson drop, and with flashing eagle eyes undimmed. He sat firmly erect, and looked in all respects more the ideal hero than in the hours of his greatest prosperity," the governor wrote.

Mrs. Davis had protested against the seizure of her pair of carriage horses, which were the gift of Richmond friends, but her protest was unheeded. "During all this wretched time," said Governor Lubbock, "she bore up with womanly fortitude. She may have expressed to her friends her indignation at the conduct of our captors, but her bearing toward them was such as to be expected from so elegant, high-souled, and refined a Southern woman. The children were all young and hovered about her like a covey of young frightened partridges.

"It was on our way East under guard that we heard the surprising news that $100,000 reward had been offered by the Washington government for the capture of the President who was accused of being an accessory to the assassination of President Lincoln, a charge so preposterous to those of us who knew him, that we were at a loss to account for its being made, until we became more fully acquainted with the blind rage that possessed the Northern people."

The President's party at this time consisted of his wife and children; Governor Lubbock; John H. Reagan, also of Texas, his Postmaster General; Col. Burton Harrison, his secretary; M. H. Clark, Acting Treasurer; Col. John Taylor Wood; Col. William Preston Johnston; and Generals [Basil Wilson] Duke, [George Gibbs] Dibrell, and W. P. C. Breckenridge, commanding the small escort. At Augusta, Georgia, there were added Vice-Pres. A. H. Stephens, Gen. Joe Wheeler, and Senator Clay of Alabama and his spirited wife.

[Clement Claiborne Clay served in the U.S. Senate before the war and in the Confederate Senate during the war.]

Vice-President Stephens and Postmaster General Reagan were sent to Fort Warren and General Wheeler, Colonel Johnston and Governor Lubbock were sent to Fort Delaware, despite the special request of the President that the Governor should be permitted to remain with him.

[Fort Warren, in Boston Harbor, Massachusetts, was used during the war for Confederate prisoners-of-war. . . . Fort Delaware, on Pea Patch Island near Delaware City, Delaware, housed as many as 12,500 Confederate prisoners, 2,700 of whom died during their incarceration.]

The President was confined at Fortress Monroe, Virginia and shackled with heavy irons. Think of it! The hero of Buena Vista, who declined President Polk's commission as brigadier general, confined to a cell and his limbs ironed to a heavy chain by Americans. But the President had said to Governor Lubbock soon after the capture that he would not make any effort to escape. There he was kept for nearly two years, Mr. Davis and his counsel all the time insisting on trial. Partisan hate all the time was seeking to secure some evidence upon which they could put him to death.

It has been said that his accusers feared to try him, for

65

fear their conviction would not stand the test of the courts; and that they secured an underground decision from the Supreme Court judges, which was that Jefferson Davis had done no more than he had a right to do under the Constitution of the United States, and it was then that they assumed a magnanimous attitude and allowed the charge to go without trial, ordering his release after two years' imprisonment.

In all his confinement and suffering, Jefferson Davis bore up as only the patriot conscious of his right-doing, and the soldier bravely facing danger and suffering, can do. Truly, his heroic conduct under such trying ordeal in defeat added a brilliance and glory to a name already sublimely great from unselfish service.

Governor Fields of Kentucky, a neutral state, in an address accepting for the state the 400-foot-high monument at Fairview, Kentucky, Jefferson Davis' birthplace — erected by loving admirers throughout the South — paid the eminent Southern leader a beautiful tribute in which he said: "The failure of the Confederacy more or less obscured the splendid qualities that belonged to this great man; but had the Confederacy been established, his name would have been second only to Washington."

[William J. Fields served thirteen years in Congress from Kentucky and became governor of that state in 1923.]

Hon. Dunbar Rowland, Mississippi's distinguished historian, in his reference to a certain class of historians and biographers, draws a distinction between a propaganda-made fame and true greatness. He says: "There is nothing more belittling to the fame of a great man than overlaudation by partial biographers. The better class of historians have discarded completely sickly sentimentality in biography. Abraham Lincoln, a strong, crude, rugged, unconventional, honest, earnest man, but a politician through-

66

out, acting his part shrewdly, has by his biographers, Nicolay and Hay, and a host of others, been transformed and elevated into a mythological hero so perfect and marvelous as to seem something of a caricature. Jefferson Davis, the equal of Lincoln in natural goodness of heart, and his superior in culture, training for statesmanship, courage, devotion to duty and earnestness of conviction, acting his part well and wisely, in failure, has received opposite treatment. He has been made the subject of bitter invective by a school of prejudiced historians who have been for many years engaged in the preparation and distribution of propaganda having no connection with truth.

"We have no need to deify Jefferson Davis; it is not necessary to indulge in extravagant eulogy, but it is incumbent upon us of the South to try to give a just historical estimate of a truly great man who was the most dominant and commanding figure in a great if not the greatest crisis in American history."

[John George Nicolay, Lincoln's private secretary, 1860-1865; coauthor with John Hay of two Lincoln books.]

As many Northern writers and speakers, notably two recent G. A. R. officials high in the councils of that organization, persist in referring to the War Between the States as a "rebellion" and the use of the word "treason" therewith, I will here quote again as appropriate Northern evidence that the war was forced upon the South by design of leading Northern men.

The *New York Herald*, April 5, 1861, said: "We have no doubt Mr. Lincoln wants the Cabinet at Montgomery to take the initiative by capturing two forts. . . . But the country and posterity will hold him just as responsible as if he struck the first blow."

Secretary of the Navy Welles: "There was not a man in the Cabinet who did not know that an attempt to reinforce Fort Sumter would be the first blow of the war."

Sen. Zack Chandler to the Governor of Michigan: "Some peace delegates here fear war, but without a little blood-letting this government will not be worth a curse. Send down some men with the fighting spirit."

Lincoln said to Editor [Joseph] Medill of Chicago [*Tribune*]: "Next to Boston, Chicago has been the chief instrument in bringing on this war. You called for war, and you got it."

The *New York Express* of April 15, 1861, said: "The people of the United States have petitioned, begged and implored these men (Lincoln, Seward, et al.) who are become their accidental masters, to give them opportunity to be heard before this unnatural strife was pushed to bloody extreme, but their petitions were spurned with contempt."

These are but a few expressions. Many could be quoted, hundreds from Northern men and Republicans. The right of the states to withdraw from the Union was recognized all through the North. Exercising that right under the Constitution, the South was not guilty of rebellion or of treason. If so, why did not the partisan Republican leaders arrest and charge with treason or fomenting rebellion the Senators and Congressmen when they resigned with avowed intention of coming South to engage in the organization of the Confederacy? Why did they not arrest and charge with treason Robert E. Lee, Stonewall Jackson, the two Johnstons, Bragg, Hood and Walker and other officers of the U.S. Army when they tendered their resignations and came to join the "rebellious" army?

[Braxton Bragg, John Bell Hood and William Henry Talbot Walker all resigned their commissions in the Union Army to become Confederate generals.]

In accepting the resignations the U.S. acknowledged the right of secession. They knew then and all the time that the Southerners were acting within their Constitutional rights. In fact the United States government had for many years taught the cadets in the Military Academy at West Point, through *Rawles' Constitution* that in event of a state withdrawing from the Union, the allegiance of the citizen or army officer was due to the state. R. E. Lee said that that instruction from that U.S. textbook left no doubt in his mind as to his duty after Virginia had seceded. Is it any wonder, when the government had so instructed, that our Southern officers resigned, or that the government so promptly accepted their resignations? There was no question of loyalty raised. But even if it were rebellion, did not George Washington, Thomas Jefferson, Patrick Henry, Ben Franklin and others renounce their allegiance to Great Britain and take up arms against that country? We applaud them. But Richmond fell!

When General Lee at Appomattox looked about him and saw the care-worn though grim-visaged and yet courageous soldiers of his army, and observed the greatly depleted ranks, while on the other hand surrounding him were the largely augmented armies of General Grant, tears dimmed his eyes. When Grant, in his several-times repeated plea for Lee's surrender, referred to the hopelessness of his situation and urged him not to fight further against the great odds opposed to him, General Lee finally yielded. The fight was lost, but not yet the cause, for Principles never die. Appomattox was a battlefield and not a forum.

# VI

# After the War

The devastation of the Southern States was so complete with four years of "reconstruction" as cruel and destructive as the war, that after it all our returning soldiers had to go to work with the same courage and determination which had characterized their conduct on the battlefield, to restore the country to its former productiveness. With what success that was done is a matter of history we are proud of. There was no time then for veteran associations and monuments, but when the Old South was again blossoming and fruiting with its pristine glory, attention was given to monuments in honor of the men who had lost in their valiant fight for the Constitution, but who had won glory on the field, and then won great renown in restored happiness and prosperity from defeat and devastation.

One of the first monuments erected was in 1886 at Montgomery, the scene of the organization of the Confederacy. Ex-Pres. Jefferson Davis accepted the invitation to be present and lay the cornerstone. In his speech he said, among other things: "Permit me to say that though the memory of our glorious past must be ever dear to us, duty points to the present and the future. Alabama having resumed her place in the Union, be it yours to fulfill all obligations devolving upon good citizens, seeking to restore the general government to its pristine purity as best you can, to promote the welfare of your common country."

His tribute to Lee on the occasion of dedicating the memorial is just as applicable to the President: "It is as much an honor to you who give as to him who receives, for above the vulgar test of merit you show yourselves competent to discriminate between him who enjoys and him who deserves success."

The time is coming when all the world will accord Davis and Lee and their compatriots the honor of being right and deserving success.

All along the way, going and returning, admiring countrymen flocked to the railway stations to get a glimpse of the great hero. All honor was paid him in Montgomery and en route. Old soldiers were overjoyed to see him again, and many shed tears of joy and gratitude as they shook his hand. In introducing Mr. Davis on that occasion Henry W. Grady said: "It is good, sir, for you to be here. Other leaders have had their triumphs. Conquerors have won crowns, and honors have been piled on the victors of earth's great battles, but never yet, sir, came man to more loving people. Never conqueror wore prouder diadem than the deathless love that crowns your grey hairs today. Never king inhabited palace more splendid than the millions of brave hearts in which your dear name and fame are forever enshrined."

[Henry W. Grady, journalist and author; editor of *Atlanta Constitution.*]

In our purpose to honor the memory of our one-time beloved leaders of the '60s and to pay tribute to the men who fought a great fight for Constitutional liberty and in

71

defense of our homes, we bear no animosity, have no bitterness in our heart. But we do insist that it is not only our blessed privilege but our sacred duty to do those things which will show the world that we respect and revere the statesmen and soldiers of the Confederacy. For my father and yours contended honestly and fearlessly for a principle — they fought for the rights of the states as guaranteed by the Federal Constitution. They not only "thought they were right," but knew they were right, and future generations of our entire country will yet acknowledge they were right.

So we have no apology to make for the course of our fathers in contending, first peacefully, under the Constitution for the right of secession, and next, in their heroic resistance to armed invasion and in defense of our homes.

Their descendants know that they honored and defended the Constitution and fought as patriots only when they were forced to arms, and that their record in peace and in war, and again in peaceful restoration of the Southland to its former glory, is a proud heritage to be preserved and honored throughout all time. Maintaining these objects can but influence a purer private life and higher public service and enhance our purpose to honor the Union and promote the welfare of our common country.

We are one country. Our loyalty has been demonstrated on a hundred battlefields since the sixties. Our purpose to honor our fathers and do what we can to perpetuate their memory is not an effort to revive animosities. No need of that. The Northerner who is so unreasonable as to criticize or the Southerner who fears it, is the disloyal and unworthy one. Contempt of brave men should be no less for the one than the other.

# VII

# Additional Highlights in History

With the purpose of showing that the excited state of mind through the Northern States in 1860 was the growth of a hundred years, beginning when slaves were owned in all the country; and was largely augmented off and on by discontents of the old Federal (monarchist) party and British influences to bring about division of our country; to throw additional light on the character of the man selected and elected to lead the prearranged campaign and to execute this violent temper of the sectional party; to contrast these combined motives with the self-sacrificial devotion of the Southern people to their high ideals of government, their devotion to principles they held dear; with further proof from Northern witnesses of the acute situation which left a self-respecting and liberty-loving people no alternative but the quiet and peaceful exercise of their Constitutional right of secession — these additional facts are presented:

There is ample authority through the history of our country that the old Federalist party was intrigued by British influences (Governor Craig of Canada and other

British representatives) with a view to help bring about a breach in the American Federation, hoping to ally New England with Great Britain.

Sir Robert Peel said that "the $100,000,000 expended to free the negroes of the West Indies was the best investment ever made for the overthrow of Republican institutions in America." The British evidently felt sure that negro equality in America would destroy our government.

[Sir James Henry Craig, Governor in Chief of Canada 1807-1811, served with the British through the American Revolution and was wounded at Bunker Hill. In 1795 he effected the capture of the Dutch colony of Cape of Good Hope, and later served in India and in the Mediterranean.... Sir Robert Peel was appointed Prime Minister of England in 1834 and again in 1841.]

One Boston paper, protesting the War of 1812 with England, declared: "We never fought to establish a republic. The form of our government was the result of necessity, and not the offspring of choice."

The *Boston Gazette* threatened President Madison with death if he compelled the Eastern States to fight against England at that time *(Horton's History,* p. 23); and Massachusetts declined to furnish her quota of troops.

John Quincy Adams, a Massachusetts man, admitted that "in New England curses and anathemas were liberally hurled from the pulpit on the heads of all those who aided, directly or indirectly, in carrying on the war" of 1812.

No less an eminent authority than Matthew Carey in his *The Olive Branch,* relates many facts in relation to a conspiracy in New England to break up the republic as early as 1796. He says: "A Northern Confederacy has been the object for a number of years. They have repeatedly advocated in public prints a separation of the states, on

74

account of pretended discordant views and interests of the different sections." (*Horton's History,* p. 11)

[Matthew Carey, Irish-American editor and publisher, who established the *Pennsylvania Herald* at Philadelphia.]

Governor Banks of Massachusetts (who, by the way, tried to invade Texas with an army of 40,000 through Louisiana, but was twice defeated and driven back to New Orleans by Gen. Dick Taylor with a third the number of Confederates), as far back as 1856, gave utterance to monarchial tendencies of his section, in declaring: "I can conceive of a time when this Constitution shall not be in existence — when we shall have an absolute dictatorial government transmitted from age to age with men at its head who are rulers by military commission, or who claim an hereditary right to govern those over whom they were placed." Just think of it! However, Lincoln made good as to the "dictatorial government" replacing the Constitutional government of our fathers.

[Nathaniel Prentiss Banks, whose choice as Speaker of the House was classed as the first national victory for the new Republican party. He served as Governor of Massachusetts from 1858 to 1861.]

William Lloyd Garrison in a public speech in the fifties declared, "This Union is a lie. The American Union is an imposture — a covenant with death, and an agreement with hell. I am for its overthrow. Up with the flag of disunion — " This from one of the founders and leaders of the Republican party.

Henry Ward Beecher and other Northern preachers furnished John Brown with rifles for his raid into Virginia

75

and spears with which to arm the negroes for insurrection. Beecher said: "It is a crime to shoot at a slave-holder and not hit him." A New England society furnished Brown money and one individual alone gave $10,000.

At a public meeting in Massachusetts, the following resolution offered by U.S. Sen. Henry Wilson was unanimously adopted: "Resolved, that it is right and the duty of slaves to resist their masters. (This when Massachusetts had grown rich on the slave traffic till stopped by Congress in 1820 by Southern votes), and the right and duty of the people of the North to incite them to resistance and to aid them in it."

At Rockford, Illinois, a public meeting "Resolved, that the city bells shall be tolled for one hour in commemoration of John Brown" — on his execution for murder in Virginia.

Another convention "resolved, that the abolitionists of this country should make it one of the primary objects of this agitation to dissolve the American Union."

The "Helper Book" so extensively circulated in Lincoln's campaign, contained over three hundred pages of vituperation and threats against the South, such as: "Do not reserve the strength of your arms until you are powerless to strike"; "We contend that slaveholders are more criminal than common murderers," and yet New England had owned slaves, and did ninety percent of the traffic in Africans whom they kidnapped in African jungles and brought over in their ships up to prohibition by the government; "The negroes, nine cases out of ten, could be delighted at the opportunity to cut their masters' throats," but what must have been their astonishment when the masters left those negro "cutthroats" to care for their wives and children for four years, and how faithfully they kept the trust!

[Hinton Rowan Helper, a native of North Carolina, was author of *The Impending Crisis of the South: How to Meet It,* published in 1857. The book attacked slavery not because it exploited the Negro, but because, the author believed, it inhibited Southern economic progress. It was widely read, especially in the North, and aroused a furor greater than that aroused by *Uncle Tom's Cabin.* One hundred thousand copies of the book were printed for use in the Republican party's 1860 Presidential campaign.]

Mr. Giddings, a prominent Ohio politician, had said: "I look forward to a day when I shall see a servile insurrection in the South; when the black man, supplied with bayonets, shall wage war of extermination against the whites — when the master shall see his dwelling in flames, and his hearth polluted, and though I may not mock their calamity and laugh when their fear cometh, yet I shall hail it as the dawn of a political millenium." But this vile dream was not realized. Even during the reconstruction period when Lincoln's followers had the South by the throat, and sent thousands of emissaries down here to bring about such a condition, they only partially succeeded for a while.

[Joshua Reed Giddings, antislavery leader, was a member of Congress from Ohio, 1838 to 1859.]

Judge Jeremiah Black, of Pennsylvania, in *Black's Essays,* said of the Federal usurpation and abuse of power under suspension of writ of habeas corpus, "Of wanton cruelties the Lincoln administration inflicted upon inoffending citizens I have neither space, nor skill, nor time, to paint them; since the fall of Robespierre, nothing has occurred to cast such disrepute upon republican institutions."

77

[Maximilien Marie Isidore Robespierre, cele-
brated French revolutionist and statesman; guil-
lotined July 28, 1794.]

Gen. Don Piatt, who traveled with Lincoln during his
campaign and knew Lincoln perhaps as well as any man,
said: "When a leader dies all good men go to lying about
him. Abraham Lincoln has almost disappeared from human
knowledge. I hear of him, I read of him in eulogies and
biographies, but fail to recognize the man I knew in life. . . .
Lincoln faced and lived through the awful responsibility
of war with a courage that came from indifference."

Ward Lamon, intimate friend of Lincoln and his U.S.
Marshal for the District of Columbia, and Colonel in the
Secret Service; Historian Shepherd of Baltimore; W. H.
Cunningham of the *Montgomery* (Missouri) *Star,* who sat
right behind Lincoln at Gettysburg, all agreed and publicly
stated that the speech published was not the one delivered
by Lincoln; that both Edward Everette and Seward expressed their disappointment and there was no applause;
that Lincoln said: "Lamon, that speech was like a wet
blanket on the audience. I am distressed about it." These
gentlemen who heard the speech all say that the speech
delivered was not the one which has been so extensively
printed. Even Nicolay says: "It was revised."

William H. Herndon, under whom Lincoln began his
law practice, and long-time friend, wrote one of the first
biographies of Lincoln, *Story of a Great Life,* but because
of its frankness in unfolding the life of Lincoln, it was
bought up and suppressed. It was republished some years
later, much modified, and from the preface this is taken:
"With a view of throwing light on some attributes of Mr.
Lincoln's character hitherto obscure these volumes are
given to the world. The whole truth concerning Mr. Lincoln should be known. The truth will at last come out,
and no man need hope to evade it. Some persons will doubtless object to the narrative of certain facts, but these facts

78

are indispensable to a full knowledge of Mr. Lincoln. We must be prepared to take Mr. Lincoln as he was. He was my warm personal friend. God's naked truth cannot injure his fame."

Lamon, in his *Life of Lincoln,* said: "The ceremony of Mr. Lincoln's apotheosis was planned and executed after his death by men who were unfriendly to him while he lived. Men who had exhausted the resources of their skill and ingenuity in venomous detractions of the living Lincoln were first after his death to undertake the task of guarding his memory, not as a human being, but as a god.

"There was a fierce rivalry as to who should canonize Mr. Lincoln in the most solemn words; who should compare him to the most sacred character in all history. He was prophet, priest, and king; he was Washington, Moses, and likened to Christ the Redeemer, and even likened unto God. After that came the ceremony of apotheosis; and this was the work of men who never spoke of the living Lincoln except with jeers and contempt. After his death it became a political necessity to pose him as the greatest, wisest, Godliest man that ever lived." Among those participating in the apotheosis Lamon names Seward, Edwin Stanton, Thad Stevens and Charles Sumner.

William Herndon says in his *Story of a Great Life*: "Lincoln detested science and literature. No man can put his finger on any book written in the last or present century that Lincoln ever read through. He read little."

Again on page 47: "When Abe saw Grigsby was getting the best of the fight (with a friend), he burst into the ring, caught Grigsby, threw him some feet distant, and then stood up, proud as Lucifer, swinging a bottle of liquor over his head and swearing aloud, 'I am the big buck of this lick; if any doubts it let him come and whet his horns.' "

Lamon, in his *Life of Lincoln,* tells the same story only adding that Grigsby challenged Lincoln to shoot with pistols, and Lincoln replied that "he was not going to fool away his life on a single shot."

These highlights from history of that period written at the time are given merely to throw additional light on the character of Abraham Lincoln, whom some insist upon characterizing a great man, and even was or would have been a friend to the South. These extracts from speeches and utterances of the leaders who organized the sectional party which nominated him for its standard-bearer, show the intense bitterness which actuated their campaign. And yet, soon after his election reflecting the sentiment or convictions these men were supposed to be fighting for, after his inauguration, upon receipt of a courteous letter from Alexander H. Stephens expressing sympathy for him in the great responsibility resting upon him as President, Lincoln wrote Mr. Stephens the following: "(For your eye only.) Do the people of the South really entertain fear that a Republican administration would directly or indirectly interfere with their slaves, or with them about their slaves? If they do, I wish to assure you as once a friend, and still, I hope, not an enemy, that there is no cause for such fears. The South would be in no more danger in this respect than it was in the days of Washington." (*Public and Private Letters of Alexander H. Stephens,* p. 150)

Isn't that a most remarkable declaration from Lincoln at such a time — and in comparison with his previous war-intent utterances and his subsequent war acts?

And yet, it seems there was such complete understanding between Washington and Boston, that Massachusetts troops were on the way even before the President's official call — true representatives of the patriots(?) who at Boston a few years before on the Fourth of July publicly burned the Constitution of the United States.

Now, one would naturally ask: If Mr. Lincoln was not contending with his party for emancipation, what was he contending for? His oft-quoted remarks about his "saving

80

the Union" is sheer bosh in view of the above and ten times more evidence that the leaders of his party were then and had for years been fighting for disunion, and destruction of the South.

Southern statesmen had been for years trying to find a fair way to free the slaves. John Randolph had freed his; R. E. Lee had liberated his; Washington, Madison, Jefferson, Mason and others endeavored to find a solution of the vexing problem which had been left with them by the British government, which had even at one time prohibited efforts to stay its advance.

[George Mason, contemporary of and coworker with Patrick Henry.]

General Lee, George Mason and Henry Clay had favored emancipation by a gradual process; and Jefferson Davis in the Senate had "urged that a plan be provided for gradual emancipation which would be best for the slave and the slaveholders." This was why Southern men were so insistent about securing more slave territory in the Northwest, so as to "relieve the congested condition in the Southern States and prepare the slaves as freed for their future government, and not have to turn them loose unprepared in the crowded Southern States, for human nature shudders at the thought of sudden emancipation." (See *Congressional Records.*)

Let us get this clear: The states were sovereign, the United States having only such powers as had been specifically delegated to the Federal confederation, mainly, to represent the states in foreign affairs, and to collect a revenue from import taxes sufficient to defray the expenses of the government, and not to protect one section or one industry at the expense of another. Jefferson Davis and other Southerners had persistently urged that peace and union could be maintained by adherence to Constitution, statutes and Supreme Court. It was Jefferson Davis who twice declined an appointment as brigadier general because the Constitution of the United States gave no such authority to the President.

*Bancroft's History,* Vol. VII, and Cooper's *American Politics,* Book IV, and other authorities give the Articles of Confederation as declaring "Each state retains its sovereignty, freedom and independence. . . ." and "all powers not expressly delegated. . . ."

As to the citizens' allegiance, both Chief Justice Chase and Horace Greeley agreed after the war that *Rawles' Constitution* (taught at West Point) and Bledsoe's *Is Davis a Traitor?* acquitted Jefferson Davis of treason, "as allegiance was due first to the State."

Chief Justice Chase said, "If Jefferson Davis is ever brought to trial it will convict the North and exonerate the South."

Responding to some friend who asked Jefferson Davis why he had not asked pardon and amnesty, he replied: "Repentance must precede right of pardon, and I have not repented. Remembering, as I must, all which has been suffered, all which has been lost, disappointed hopes and crushed aspirations, yet I deliberately say, if it were to do over again, I would do just as I did in 1861. Never teach your children that their fathers were wrong in their efforts to maintain the sovereignty, freedom and independence which was their inalienable birthright. I cannot believe that the causes for which our sacrifices were made can ever be lost, but rather hope that those who now deny the justice of our asserted claims will learn from experience that the fathers builded wisely and the Constitution should be construed according to the commentaries of those men who made it."

# Index

84